RAMADAN
Activity Book

- Journal
- Planner
- Coloring
- Mazes
- Word Searsh
- Drawing
- Copy the picture
- Knowledge

THIS BOOK BELONGS TO:

NAME: ______________________________

DATE OF BIRTH: ______________________________

RAMADAN DATE: ______________________________

Assalamu Alaikum Dear

Thank you for using our Ramadan activity book for kids.
It's great to see that you enjoy doing these activities as much as we do!

This is a perfect workbook! It has been designed for you to make sure that you have all the activities you could want at any time during the days of Ramadan.
It will provide hours of gratitude-planning and tracking, entertainment, and a refreshing way to separate and improve your brain function through coloring, hand-eye coordination, problem-solving and more!

Let's start with bismillah

Ramadan Day 1

Date: ....

Color in prayer "sajada" for each salah you perform today

Fajr	Duhr	Asr	Maghrib	Isha
2	4	4	3	4

My Quran Tracker

Surah: ....

Verse: .... to: ....
Verse: .... to: ....
Verse: .... to: ....
Verse: .... to: ....
Verse: .... to: ....

My Dhikr Tracker

- Astaghfirullah: ....
- Subhan Allah: ....
- Alhamdulillah: ....
- la ilaha illa llah: ....
- Allahu Akbar: ....

My Good Deeds Checklist

- I Eat Sahour
- I Say Only Good Things
- I Make my Parents Happy
- I Did Dhikr
- I Give Sadaqah
- I Keep my Room Tidy
- I Help Set Up the Table of Iftar
- I Read Lots About Islam
- I Read lots of Al-Quran
- I Prayer on Time

My Fasting Was:

Part Half Most Full

My Thoughts:

....
....
....
....
....

Doodle Challenge for Today

Draw and label 2 Different Kinds of: Mushrooms

Activity for Today

Search for the Crescent Moon
In The sky this evening

COPY THE PICTURE

	A	B	C	D	E	F
1						
2						
3						
4						
5						
6						
7						
8						

Ramadan Day 2 Date: ....

Color in prayer "sajada" for each salah you perform today

Fajr	Duhr	Asr	Maghrib	Isha
2	4	4	3	4

My Quran Tracker

Surah: ....

Verse: .... to: ....
Verse: .... to: ....
Verse: .... to: ....
Verse: .... to: ....
Verse: .... to: ....

My Dhikr Tracker

- ♡ Astaghfirullah: ....
- ♡ Subhan Allah: ....
- ♡ Alhamdulillah: ....
- ♡ la ilaha illa llah: ....
- ♡ Allahu Akbar: ....

My Good Deeds Checklist

- ♡ I Eat Sahour
- ♡ I Say Only Good Things
- ♡ I Make my Parents Happy
- ♡ I Did Dhikr
- ♡ I Give Sadaqah
- ♡ I Keep my Room Tidy
- ♡ I Help Set Up the Table of Iftar
- ♡ I Read Lots About Islam
- ♡ I Read lots of Al-Quran
- ♡ I Prayer on Time

My Fasting Was:

☆ Part ☆ Half ☆ Most ☆ Full

My Thoughts:

....

Cut and Color this picture

Al Kaaba - Baitullah al haram

Doodle Challenge for Today

Draw and label 2 Different Kinds of: Houses

Activity for Today

Read the sermon of the prophet Muhammad "Sala-llahu-alihi-wasalam"

Word Search

Search and find the five words

W	A	R	W	U	H	A	B	A	K	K
I	C	I	Y	Y	S	U	G	N	K	Z
P	N	Q	B	A	Q	L	W	K	X	Z
D	H	Y	W	R	X	E	D	E	G	O
I	A	Y	D	J	D	U	Z	V	E	R
N	N	C	D	Y	O	N	M	M	P	V
Z	A	X	N	D	K	E	H	T	M	F
A	M	I	Z	D	O	P	B	X	T	X
K	A	S	R	N	S	N	G	Z	L	Z
S	B	Q	M	S	M	F	Z	E	B	I
Z	N	B	C	K	T	H	I	J	R	A
F	R	D	I	W	A	Y	O	B	C	F
M	C	B	I	R	H	G	A	M	U	E

AMANAH **DIN** **HIJRA**

KABAH **MAGHRIB**

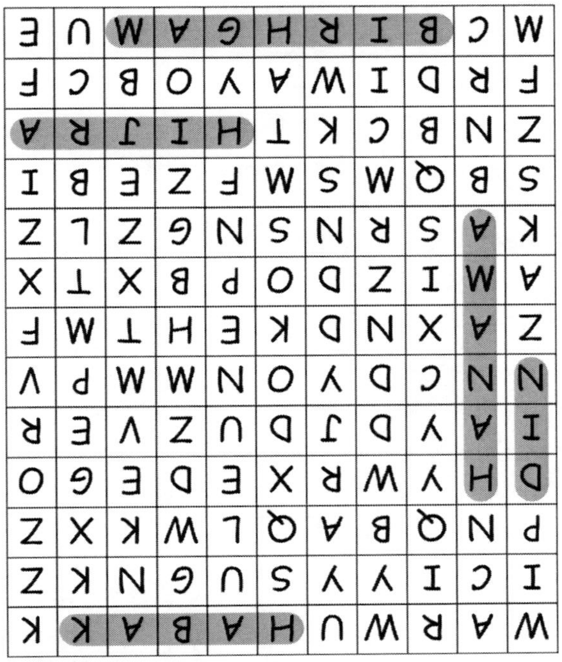

THE SOLUTION

AMANAH

the trust. Of all creation, only human beings & jinns carry the "trust", which is free will

DIN

(literally 'religion') the way of life based on Islamic revelation; the sum total of a Muslim's faith and practice.

HIJRA

Muhammad "Sala-allahu-alihi-wasalam" and his followers' emigration from Mecca to Medina.

KABAH

cube-house; i.e., the cube-shaped building in Mecca which Muslims face to pray.

MAGHRIB

the fourth daily salat prayer

Ramadan Day 3 Date: ....

Color in prayer "sajada" for each salah you perform today

Fajr	Duhr	Asr	Maghrib	Isha
2	4	4	3	4

My Quran Tracker

Surah: ....

Verse: .... to: ....
Verse: .... to: ....
Verse: .... to: ....
Verse: .... to: ....
Verse: .... to: ....

My Dhikr Tracker

- Astaghfirullah: ....
- Subhan Allah: ....
- Alhamdulillah: ....
- la ilaha illa llah: ....
- Allahu Akbar: ....

My Good Deeds Checklist

- I Eat Sahour
- I Say Only Good Things
- I Make my Parents Happy
- I Did Dhikr
- I Give Sadaqah
- I Keep my Room Tidy
- I Help Set Up the Table of Iftar
- I Read Lots About Islam
- I Read lots of Al-Quran
- I Prayer on Time

My Fasting Was:

Part Half Most Full

My Thoughts: ....

Doodle Challenge for Today

Draw and label 2 Different Kinds of: Cakes

Activity for Today

Make a calendar chain

Everything is Fine,
and Anything is Possible.

MAZE PUZZLE

Can you help dad find the car keys

Ramadan Day 4 Date: ....

Color in prayer "sajada" for each salah you perform today

Fajr	Duhr	Asr	Maghrib	Isha
2	4	4	3	4

My Quran Tracker

Surah: ....

Verse: .... to: ....
Verse: .... to: ....
Verse: .... to: ....
Verse: .... to: ....
Verse: .... to: ....

My Dhikr Tracker

- ♡ Astaghfirullah: ....
- ♡ Subhan Allah: ....
- ♡ Alhamdulillah: ....
- ♡ la ilaha illa llah: ....
- ♡ Allahu Akbar: ....

My Good Deeds Checklist

- ♡ I Eat Sahour
- ♡ I Say Only Good Things
- ♡ I Make my Parents Happy
- ♡ I Did Dhikr
- ♡ I Give Sadaqah
- ♡ I Keep my Room Tidy
- ♡ I Help Set Up the Table of Iftar
- ♡ I Read Lots About Islam
- ♡ I Read lots of Al-Quran
- ♡ I Prayer on Time

My Fasting Was:

Part Half Most Full

My Thoughts: ....

....

....

....

....

Doodle Challenge for Today

Draw and label 2 Different Kinds of: Red Fruit

Activity for Today

Gather some books to read

Word Search

Search and find the five words

Z	N	L	H	H	A	K	A	R	A	B
X	Z	K	B	G	P	L	G	W	I	T
I	H	P	V	Q	Z	D	X	L	R	C
U	L	E	W	M	W	I	D	Q	D	Z
R	Q	R	K	I	H	D	U	A	B	E
W	N	B	F	Z	S	H	T	V	H	L
Q	S	R	M	L	T	H	U	K	S	P
U	M	I	B	A	K	F	A	J	R	P
Z	P	F	S	D	Q	R	F	B	J	Y
Q	E	T	Q	H	B	N	A	F	L	Y
Q	C	A	K	A	L	Z	O	Y	J	D
Y	V	R	I	N	K	G	N	R	K	R
D	V	T	F	C	I	N	Y	O	H	S

ADHAN **BARAKAH** **DHIKR**

FAJR **IFTAR**

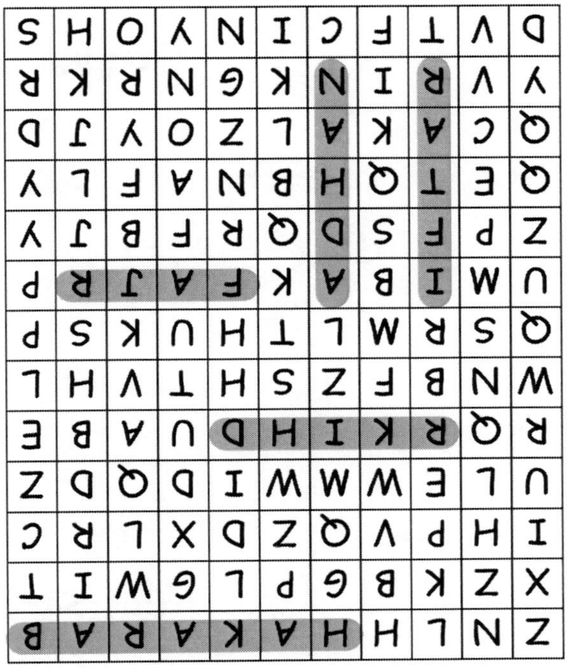

THE SOLUTION

ADHAN

**call to salat (prayer),
sometimes alternatively spelled and pronounced Azaan,
Athaan and Adhan**

BARAKAH

**a form of blessing, thought derive from God and
passed on others via prophets,
angels and saints.**

DHIKR

**A devotional practice whereby the name of God
is repeated in a rhythmical manner.**

FAJR

**dawn, early morning, and the morning prayer.
The time of the day when there is light in the horizon before sunrise.**

IFTAR

**a meal eaten by Muslims breaking their fast
after sunset during the month of Ramadan.**

Ramadan Day 5

Date: ....

Color in prayer "sajada" for each salah you perform today

Fajr	Duhr	Asr	Maghrib	Isha
2	4	4	3	4

My Quran Tracker

Surah: ....

Verse: .... to: ....
Verse: .... to: ....
Verse: .... to: ....
Verse: .... to: ....
Verse: .... to: ....

My Dhikr Tracker

- ♡ Astaghfirullah: ....
- ♡ Subhan Allah: ....
- ♡ Alhamdulillah: ....
- ♡ la ilaha illa llah: ....
- ♡ Allahu Akbar: ....

My Good Deeds Checklist

- ♡ I Eat Sahour
- ♡ I Say Only Good Things
- ♡ I Make my Parents Happy
- ♡ I Did Dhikr
- ♡ I Give Sadaqah
- ♡ I Keep my Room Tidy
- ♡ I Help Set Up the Table of Iftar
- ♡ I Read Lots About Islam
- ♡ I Read lots of Al-Quran
- ♡ I Prayer on Time

My Fasting Was:

☆ Part ☆ Half ☆ Most ☆ Full

My Thoughts:

....

....

....

....

....

Doodle Challenge for Today

Draw and label 2 Different Kinds of: Shoes

Activity for Today

Write letter to friends or relatives

COPY THE PICTURE

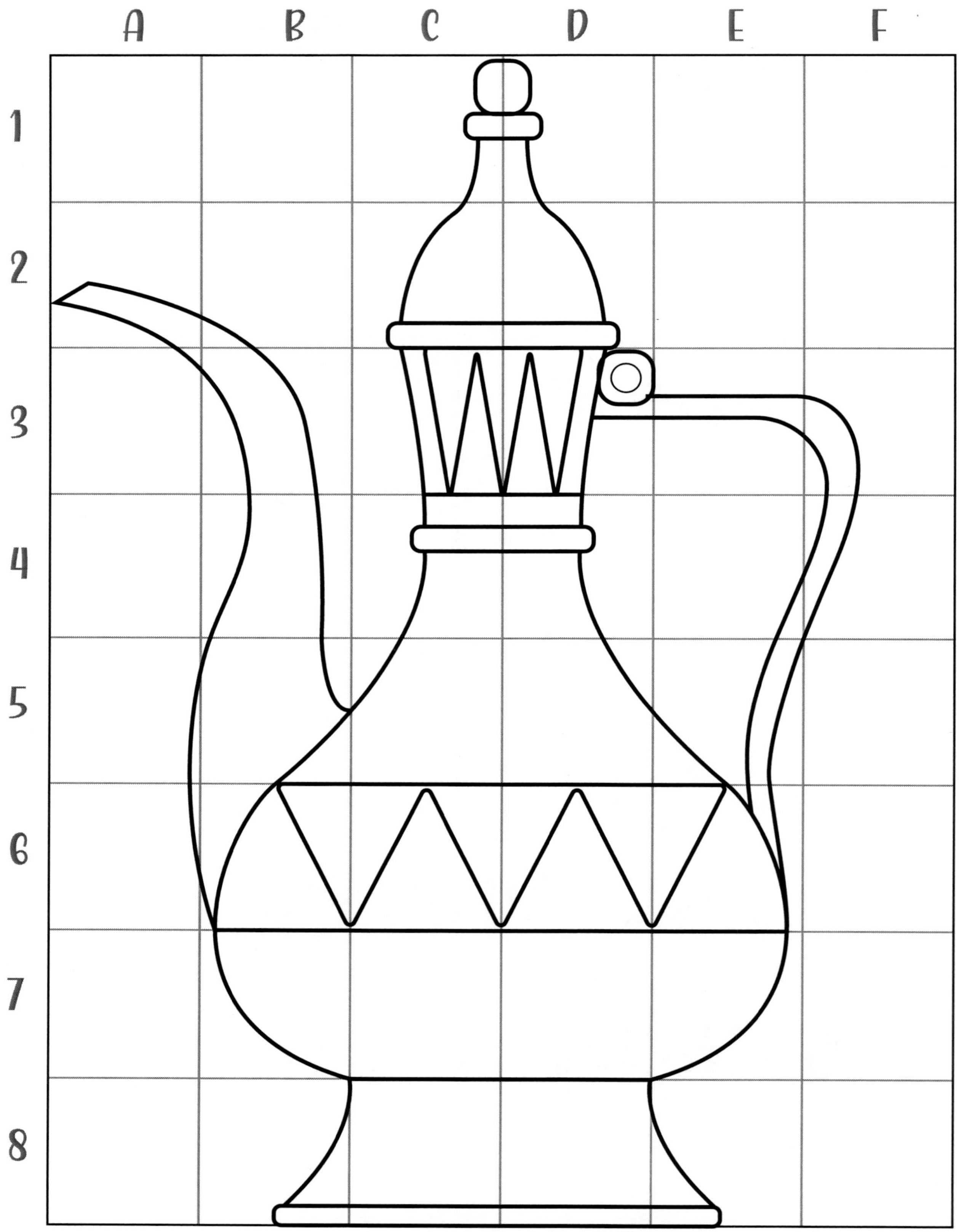

	A	B	C	D	E	F
1						
2						
3						
4						
5						
6						
7						
8						

Ramadan Day 6 Date: ....

Color in prayer "sajada" for each salah you perform today

Fajr	Duhr	Asr	Maghrib	Isha
2	4	4	3	4

My Quran Tracker

Surah: ....

Verse: .... to: ....
Verse: .... to: ....
Verse: .... to: ....
Verse: .... to: ....
Verse: .... to: ....

My Dhikr Tracker

- ♡ Astaghfirullah: ....
- ♡ Subhan Allah: ....
- ♡ Alhamdulillah: ....
- ♡ la ilaha illa llah: ....
- ♡ Allahu Akbar: ....

My Good Deeds Checklist

- ♡ I Eat Sahour
- ♡ I Say Only Good Things
- ♡ I Make my Parents Happy
- ♡ I Did Dhikr
- ♡ I Give Sadaqah
- ♡ I Keep my Room Tidy
- ♡ I Help Set Up the Table of Iftar
- ♡ I Read Lots About Islam
- ♡ I Read lots of Al-Quran
- ♡ I Prayer on Time

My Fasting Was:

Part Half Most Full

My Thoughts:

....

Cut and Color this picture

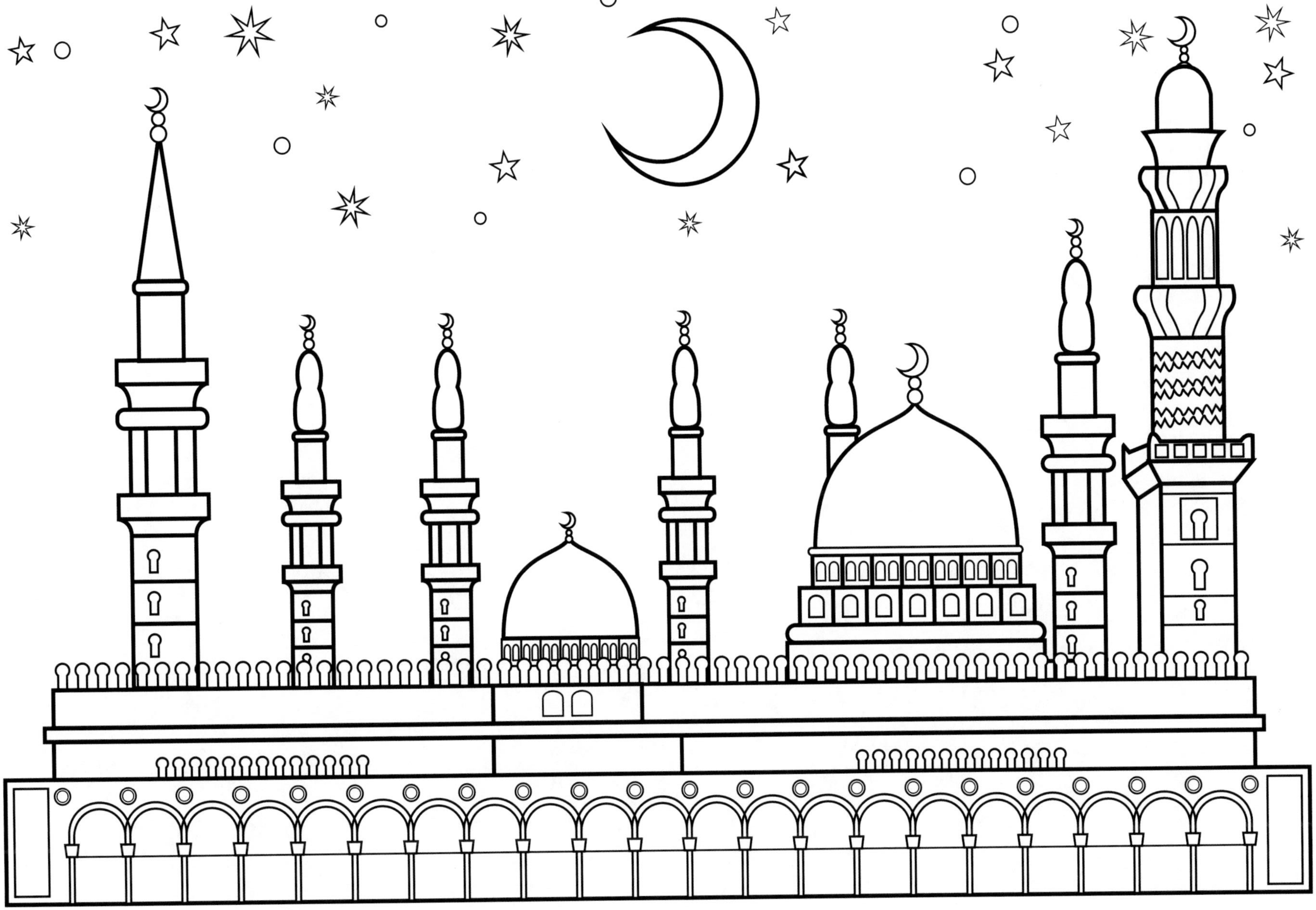

Al Masjid Al Nabawi

Doodle Challenge for Today

Draw and label 2 Different Kinds of: Cars

Activity for Today

Practise dribbling a Ball with each hand for 5 minute

Word Search

Search and find the five words

Q	C	K	D	Y	O	X	P	D	W	M
F	Q	R	Y	Z	D	R	F	T	Z	J
P	A	H	S	I	H	T	F	Y	D	I
I	Q	P	K	D	O	N	Q	A	N	T
X	P	S	E	D	I	J	S	A	M	L
H	F	A	Y	V	L	H	E	X	R	M
L	V	A	C	C	E	M	N	E	I	C
H	A	N	N	A	J	R	M	Z	H	H
S	D	S	C	Y	J	S	S	B	J	I
B	L	N	B	T	I	W	E	E	Q	L
B	W	S	I	B	K	F	W	M	G	A
C	B	G	M	X	P	Y	N	G	Y	L
P	G	A	K	T	I	L	V	V	N	C

JANNAH **MASJID** **MECCA**

ISHA **HILAL**

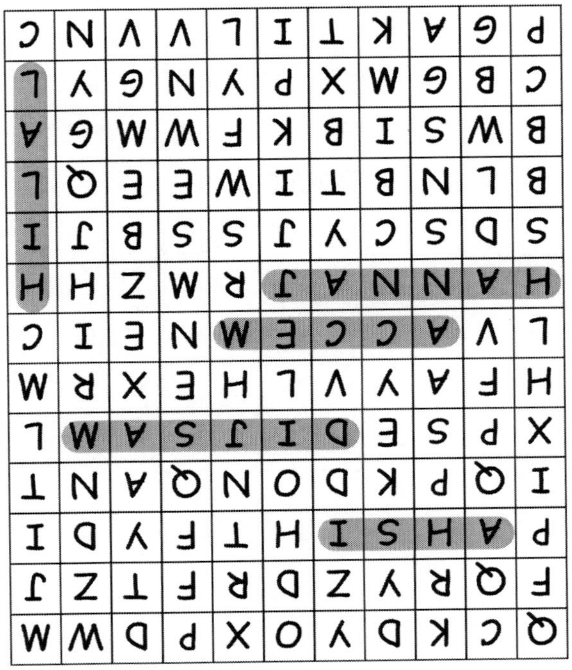

THE SOLUTION

JANNAH

Paradise, Heaven, the Garden

MASJID

Place of prayer; mosque

MACCA

The holiest city in Islam

ISHA

Night. the fifth salat prayer

HILAL

Crescent moon.

Ramadan Day 7 Date: ....

Color in prayer "sajada" for each salah you perform today

Fajr	Duhr	Asr	Maghrib	Isha
2	4	4	3	4

My Quran Tracker

Surah: ....

Verse: .... to: ....
Verse: .... to: ....
Verse: .... to: ....
Verse: .... to: ....
Verse: .... to: ....

My Dhikr Tracker

- Astaghfirullah: ....
- Subhan Allah: ....
- Alhamdulillah: ....
- la ilaha illa llah: ....
- Allahu Akbar: ....

My Good Deeds Checklist

- I Eat Sahour
- I Say Only Good Things
- I Make my Parents Happy
- I Did Dhikr
- I Give Sadaqah
- I Keep my Room Tidy
- I Help Set Up the Table of Iftar
- I Read Lots About Islam
- I Read lots of Al-Quran
- I Prayer on Time

My Fasting Was:

Part Half Most Full

My Thoughts:

....
....
....
....
....

Doodle Challenge for Today

Draw and label 2 Different Kinds of: Trees

Activity for Today

Surprise your parents by vacuuming the rugs

It is enough to do your best,
You can do it.

MAZE PUZZLE

Can you help the mother make the soup

Ramadan Day 8

Date: ....

Color in prayer "sajada" for each salah you perform today

Fajr	Duhr	Asr	Maghrib	Isha
2	4	4	3	4

My Quran Tracker

Surah: ....

Verse: .... to: ....
Verse: .... to: ....
Verse: .... to: ....
Verse: .... to: ....
Verse: .... to: ....

My Dhikr Tracker

- Astaghfirullah: ....
- Subhan Allah: ....
- Alhamdulillah: ....
- la ilaha illa llah: ....
- Allahu Akbar: ....

My Good Deeds Checklist

- I Eat Sahour
- I Say Only Good Things
- I Make my Parents Happy
- I Did Dhikr
- I Give Sadaqah
- I Keep my Room Tidy
- I Help Set Up the Table of Iftar
- I Read Lots About Islam
- I Read lots of Al-Quran
- I Prayer on Time

My Fasting Was:

Part Half Most Full

My Thoughts:

....
....
....
....
....

Doodle Challenge for Today

Draw and label 2 Different Kinds of: Nuts

Activity for Today

Juggle an inflated freezer bag or football

Word Search

Search and find the five words

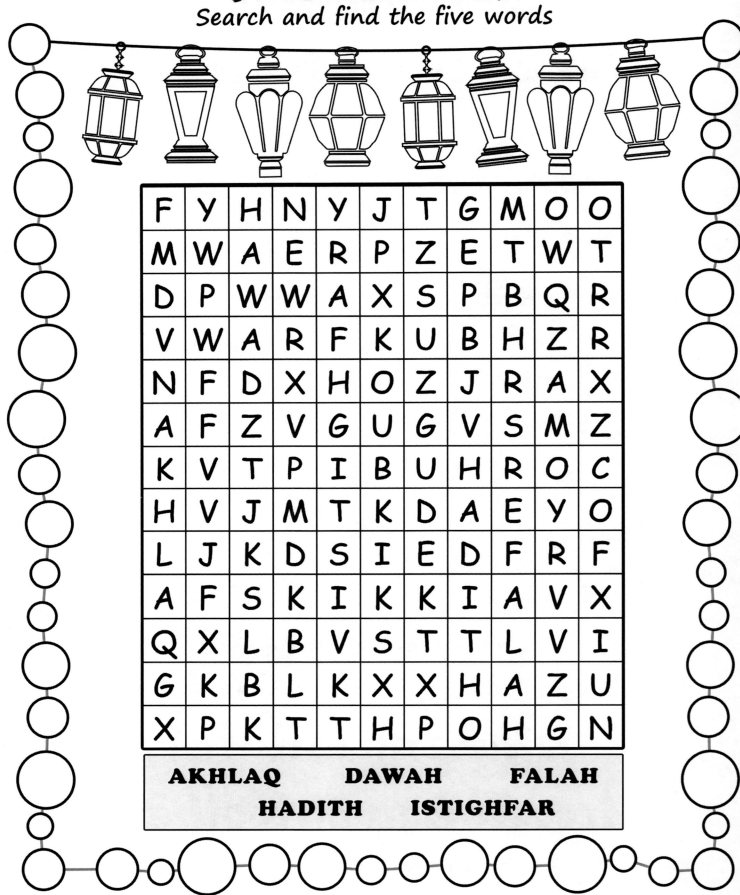

F	Y	H	N	Y	J	T	G	M	O	O
M	W	A	E	R	P	Z	E	T	W	T
D	P	W	W	A	X	S	P	B	Q	R
V	W	A	R	F	K	U	B	H	Z	R
N	F	D	X	H	O	Z	J	R	A	X
A	F	Z	V	G	U	G	V	S	M	Z
K	V	T	P	I	B	U	H	R	O	C
H	V	J	M	T	K	D	A	E	Y	O
L	J	K	D	S	I	E	D	F	R	F
A	F	S	K	I	K	K	I	A	V	X
Q	X	L	B	V	S	T	T	L	V	I
G	K	B	L	K	X	X	H	A	Z	U
X	P	K	T	T	H	P	O	H	G	N

AKHLAQ **DAWAH** **FALAH**

HADITH **ISTIGHFAR**

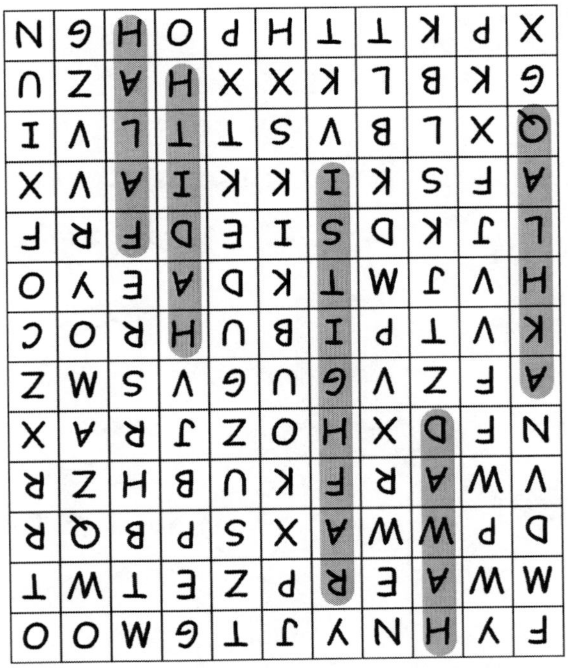

THE SOLUTION

AKHLAQ

The practice of virtue. Morals.

DAWAH

The call to Islam

FALAH

Deliverance, salvation, well-being.

HADITH

Literally "speech"; recorded saying or tradition of Muhammad "Sala-allahu-alih-wasalam"validated by isnad; with sira these comprise the sunnah and reveal shariah

---

ISTIGHFAR

Requesting forgiveness

Ramadan Day 9

Date: ....

Color in prayer "sajada" for each salah you perform today

Fajr	Duhr	Asr	Maghrib	Isha
2	4	4	3	4

My Quran Tracker

Surah: ....

Verse: .... to: ....
Verse: .... to: ....
Verse: .... to: ....
Verse: .... to: ....
Verse: .... to: ....

My Dhikr Tracker

- Astaghfirullah: ....
- Subhan Allah: ....
- Alhamdulillah: ....
- la ilaha illa llah: ....
- Allahu Akbar: ....

My Good Deeds Checklist

- I Eat Sahour
- I Say Only Good Things
- I Make my Parents Happy
- I Did Dhikr
- I Give Sadaqah
- I Keep my Room Tidy
- I Help Set Up the Table of Iftar
- I Read Lots About Islam
- I Read lots of Al-Quran
- I Prayer on Time

My Fasting Was:

Part · Half · Most · Full

My Thoughts:

....
....
....
....
....

Doodle Challenge for Today

Draw and label 2 Different Kinds of: Blue thing

Activity for Today

Build a fort with a couch cushion and pillows

COPY THE PICTURE

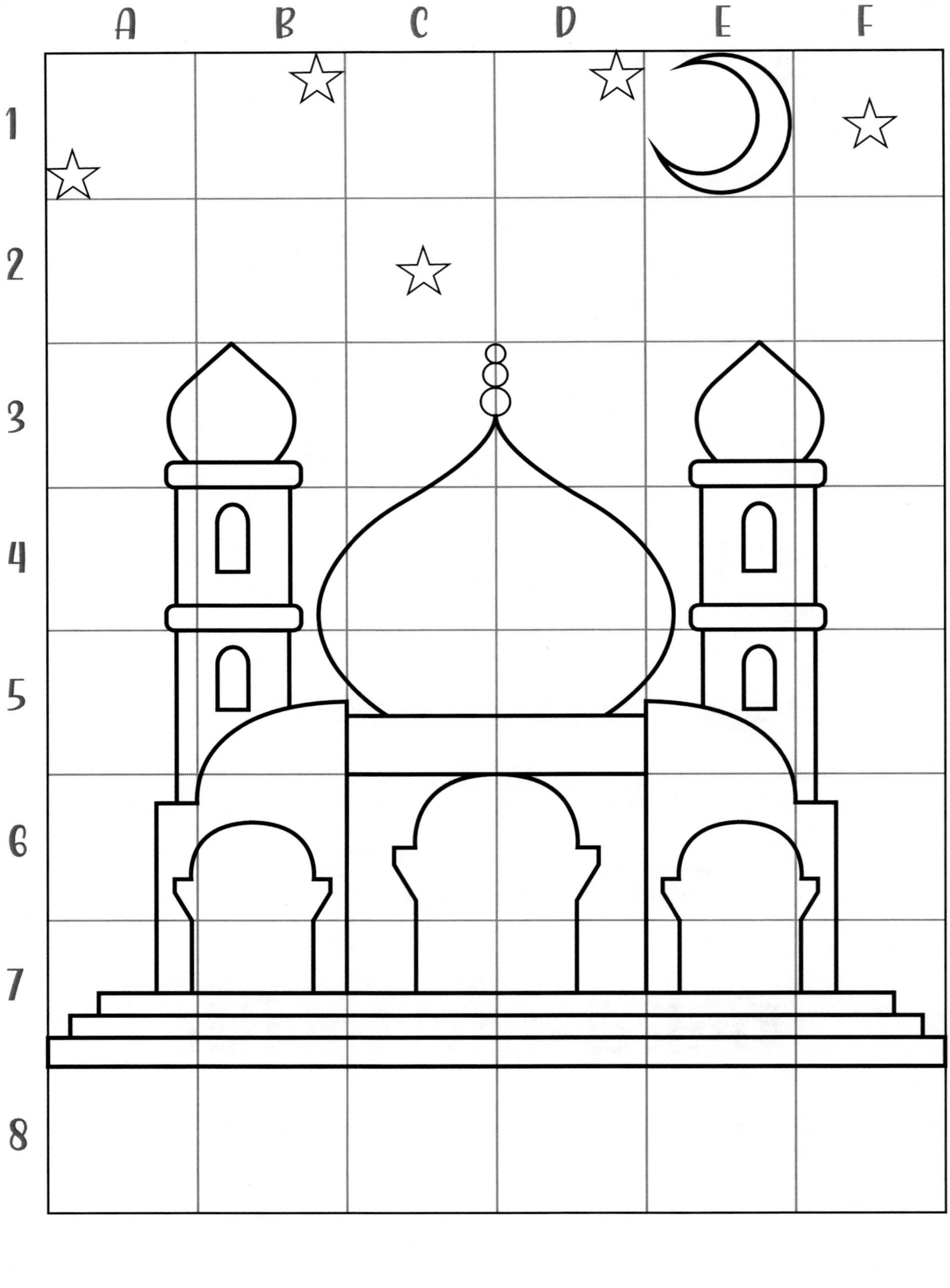

	A	B	C	D	E	F
1						
2						
3						
4						
5						
6						
7						
8						

Ramadan Day 10

Date: ....

Color in prayer "sajada" for each salah you perform today

Fajr	Duhr	Asr	Maghrib	Isha
2	4	4	3	4

My Quran Tracker

Surah: ....

Verse: .... to: ....
Verse: .... to: ....
Verse: .... to: ....
Verse: .... to: ....
Verse: .... to: ....

My Dhikr Tracker

- ♡ Astaghfirullah: ....
- ♡ Subhan Allah: ....
- ♡ Alhamdulillah: ....
- ♡ la ilaha illa llah: ....
- ♡ Allahu Akbar: ....

My Good Deeds Checklist

- ♡ I Eat Sahour
- ♡ I Say Only Good Things
- ♡ I Make my Parents Happy
- ♡ I Did Dhikr
- ♡ I Give Sadaqah
- ♡ I Keep my Room Tidy
- ♡ I Help Set Up the Table of Iftar
- ♡ I Read Lots About Islam
- ♡ I Read lots of Al-Quran
- ♡ I Prayer on Time

My Fasting Was:

☆ Part ☆ Half ☆ Most ☆ Full

My Thoughts:

....

....

....

....

....

Cut and Color this picture

Al Masjid Al Aqsa

Doodle Challenge for Today

Draw and label 2 Different Kinds of: Toys

Activity for Today

How many stacked pillows can you jump over. ______

Ramadan Day 11 Date: ....

Color in prayer "sajada" for each salah you perform today

Fajr	Duhr	Asr	Maghrib	Isha
2	4	4	3	4

My Quran Tracker

Surah: ....

Verse: .... to: ....
Verse: .... to: ....
Verse: .... to: ....
Verse: .... to: ....
Verse: .... to: ....

My Dhikr Tracker

- ♡ Astaghfirullah: ....
- ♡ Subhan Allah: ....
- ♡ Alhamdulillah: ....
- ♡ la ilaha illa llah: ....
- ♡ Allahu Akbar: ....

My Good Deeds Checklist

- ♡ I Eat Sahour
- ♡ I Say Only Good Things
- ♡ I Make my Parents Happy
- ♡ I Did Dhikr
- ♡ I Give Sadaqah
- ♡ I Keep my Room Tidy
- ♡ I Help Set Up the Table of Iftar
- ♡ I Read Lots About Islam
- ♡ I Read lots of Al-Quran
- ♡ I Prayer on Time

My Fasting Was:

Part Half Most Full

My Thoughts: ....

....

....

....

....

Doodle Challenge for Today

Draw and label 2 Different Kinds of: Seashells

Activity for Today

Prepare goals for the next month

Word Search

Search and find the five words

A	O	Z	O	R	D	U	T	K	H	B
I	C	C	W	U	N	L	X	Y	L	X
A	I	V	Z	I	R	D	F	Z	P	K
L	N	C	C	O	Y	Y	O	M	E	T
N	I	H	C	G	X	L	B	Z	H	J
R	Z	V	T	U	S	A	L	T	I	Q
K	N	R	F	Y	O	L	B	O	M	B
X	I	A	M	A	R	A	H	J	I	Y
M	S	S	G	J	X	H	X	P	M	R
O	L	N	W	T	I	O	X	M	I	C
L	A	A	H	C	M	A	T	Q	I	D
I	M	E	D	N	A	M	E	A	M	A
J	J	D	B	W	N	L	D	B	D	V

HARAM **HALAL** **IMAN**

ANSAR **ISLAM**

THE SOLUTION

A	O	Z	O	R	D	U	T	K	H	B
I	C	C	M	U	N	L	X	Y	L	X
A	I	V	Z	I	R	D	F	Z	P	K
L	N	C	C	O	Y	Y	O	M	E	T
N	I	H	C	G	X	L	B	Z	H	J
R	Z	V	T	U	S	A	L	T	I	Q
K	N	R	F	Y	O	L	B	O	M	B
X	I	A	M	A	R	A	H	J	I	Y
M	S	S	G	J	X	H	X	P	M	R
O	L	N	M	T	I	O	X	M	I	C
L	A	A	H	C	M	A	T	Q	I	D
I	M	E	D	N	A	M	E	A	M	A
J	J	D	B	M	N	L	D	B	D	A

HARAM

Sinful

HALAL

Lawful, permitted, good, beneficial, praiseworthy, honorable.

IMAN

Personal faith

ANSAR

"Helpers." The Muslim converts at Medina who helped the Muslims from Mecca after the Hijrah.

ISLAM

"submission to God". The Arabic root word for Islam means submission, obedience, peace, and purity.

Ramadan Day 12

Date: ....

Color in prayer "sajada" for each salah you perform today

Fajr	Duhr	Asr	Maghrib	Isha
2	4	4	3	4

My Quran Tracker

Surah: ....

Verse: .... to: ....
Verse: .... to: ....
Verse: .... to: ....
Verse: .... to: ....
Verse: .... to: ....

My Dhikr Tracker

- Astaghfirullah: ....
- Subhan Allah: ....
- Alhamdulillah: ....
- la ilaha illa llah: ....
- Allahu Akbar: ....

My Good Deeds Checklist

- I Eat Sahour
- I Say Only Good Things
- I Make my Parents Happy
- I Did Dhikr
- I Give Sadaqah
- I Keep my Room Tidy
- I Help Set Up the Table of Iftar
- I Read Lots About Islam
- I Read lots of Al-Quran
- I Prayer on Time

My Fasting Was:

Part / Half / Most / Full

My Thoughts:

....

Doodle Challenge for Today

Draw and label 2 Different Kinds of: Palm

Activity for Today

learn about the moon phases

You must engage in small acts of kindness to uplift other people

MAZE PUZZLE

Can you help someone in need of Zakat Al-Fitr?

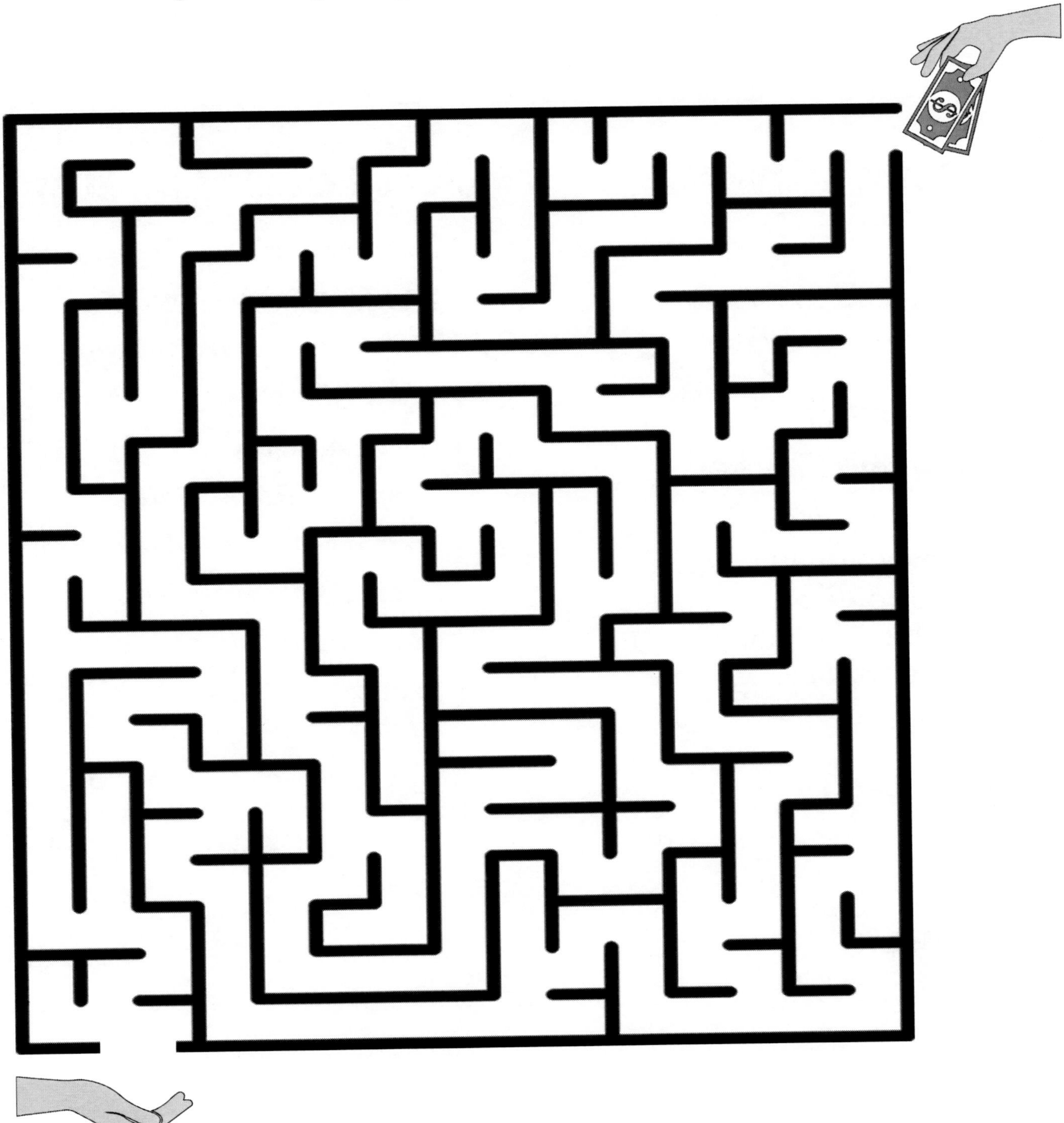

Ramadan Day 13 Date: ....

Color in prayer "sajada" for each salah you perform today

Fajr	Duhr	Asr	Maghrib	Isha
2	4	4	3	4

My Quran Tracker

Surah: ....

Verse: .... to: ....
Verse: .... to: ....
Verse: .... to: ....
Verse: .... to: ....
Verse: .... to: ....

My Dhikr Tracker

- ♡ Astaghfirullah: ....
- ♡ Subhan Allah: ....
- ♡ Alhamdulillah: ....
- ♡ la ilaha illa llah: ....
- ♡ Allahu Akbar: ....

My Good Deeds Checklist

- ♡ I Eat Sahour
- ♡ I Say Only Good Things
- ♡ I Make my Parents Happy
- ♡ I Did Dhikr
- ♡ I Give Sadaqah
- ♡ I Keep my Room Tidy
- ♡ I Help Set Up the Table of Iftar
- ♡ I Read Lots About Islam
- ♡ I Read lots of Al-Quran
- ♡ I Prayer on Time

My Fasting Was:

☆ Part ☆ Half ☆ Most ☆ Full

My Thoughts:

....

Doodle Challenge for Today

Draw and label 2 Different Kinds of: Leaves

Activity for Today

Make a lantern

Word Search

Search and find the five words

V	S	D	U	J	N	V	B	W	D	L
K	T	Q	Q	I	D	H	H	A	J	J
U	B	X	W	V	P	V	B	W	R	F
T	J	D	K	L	I	R	B	Y	N	L
T	M	I	R	A	J	K	V	F	I	A
A	A	P	B	S	H	C	U	T	U	R
I	T	T	A	Q	U	L	L	A	H	A
V	R	F	I	S	R	A	G	Q	P	M
X	F	W	C	F	F	I	W	X	I	J
L	J	E	K	D	A	K	L	V	I	Z
R	A	K	H	I	R	A	H	Z	K	O
R	Y	U	C	Z	A	F	C	I	S	E
F	P	F	E	V	G	J	J	Q	R	Z

AKHIRAH **HAJJ** **ISRA**

MIRAJ **ITTAQULLAH**

THE SOLUTION

V	S	D	U	J	N	V	B	W	D	L
K	T	Q	Q	I	D	H	H	A	J	J
U	B	X	W	V	P	V	B	W	R	F
T	J	D	K	L	I	R	B	Y	N	L
T	W	I	R	A	J	K	V	F	I	A
A	A	P	B	S	H	C	U	T	U	R
I	T	T	A	Q	U	L	L	A	H	A
V	R	F	I	S	R	A	G	Q	P	M
X	F	W	C	F	F	I	W	X	I	J
L	J	E	K	D	A	K	L	V	I	Z
R	A	K	H	I	R	A	H	Z	K	O
R	Y	U	C	Z	A	F	C	I	S	E
F	P	F	E	V	G	J	J	Q	R	Z

AKHIRAH

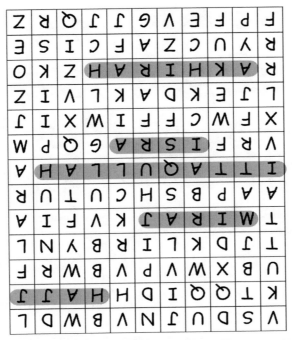

Hereafter or eternal life

HAJJ

Pilgrimage to Mecca. It's the fifth Pillar of Islam

ISRA

The night that the Prophet Muhammad "sala-llahu-alaihi-wasalam", traveled from Mecca to Al-Aqsa Mosque in Palestine

MIRAJ

On the same night as the Night Journey ...The Mi'raj means ascending to the seven heavens

ITAQULLAH

Command to fear God or to be pious to Allah

Ramadan Day 14 Date: ....

Color in prayer "sajada" for each salah you perform today

Fajr	Duhr	Asr	Maghrib	Isha
2	4	4	3	4

My Quran Tracker

Surah: ....

Verse: .... to: ....
Verse: .... to: ....
Verse: .... to: ....
Verse: .... to: ....
Verse: .... to: ....

My Dhikr Tracker

- Astaghfirullah: ....
- Subhan Allah: ....
- Alhamdulillah: ....
- la ilaha illa llah: ....
- Allahu Akbar: ....

My Good Deeds Checklist

- I Eat Sahour
- I Say Only Good Things
- I Make my Parents Happy
- I Did Dhikr
- I Give Sadaqah
- I Keep my Room Tidy
- I Help Set Up the Table of Iftar
- I Read Lots About Islam
- I Read lots of Al-Quran
- I Prayer on Time

My Fasting Was:

Part Half Most Full

My Thoughts:

....

Doodle Challenge for Today

Draw and label 2 Different Kinds of: Vehicles

Activity for Today

Design a ramadan T-shirt

COPY THE PICTURE

	A	B	C	D	E	F
1						
2						
3						
4						
5						
6						
7						
8						

Ramadan Day 15 Date: ....

Color in prayer "sajada" for each salah you perform today

Fajr	Duhr	Asr	Maghrib	Isha
2	4	4	3	4

My Quran Tracker

Surah: ....

Verse: .... to: ....
Verse: .... to: ....
Verse: .... to: ....
Verse: .... to: ....
Verse: .... to: ....

My Dhikr Tracker

- ♡ Astaghfirullah: ....
- ♡ Subhan Allah: ....
- ♡ Alhamdulillah: ....
- ♡ la ilaha illa llah: ....
- ♡ Allahu Akbar: ....

My Good Deeds Checklist

- ♡ I Eat Sahour
- ♡ I Say Only Good Things
- ♡ I Make my Parents Happy
- ♡ I Did Dhikr
- ♡ I Give Sadaqah
- ♡ I Keep my Room Tidy
- ♡ I Help Set Up the Table of Iftar
- ♡ I Read Lots About Islam
- ♡ I Read lots of Al-Quran
- ♡ I Prayer on Time

My Fasting Was:

Part Half Most Full

My Thoughts:

....
....
....
....
....

Cut and Color this picture

Qubbat Al Sakhra

Doodle Challenge for Today

Draw and label 2 Different Kinds of: Green things

Activity for Today

Make a bookmark

Word Search

Search and find the five words

H	J	O	U	T	Y	U	B	K	W	C
D	T	A	Z	P	U	K	A	Z	R	E
I	J	A	I	A	Z	K	K	R	W	G
Y	O	N	G	A	J	M	P	P	B	N
P	L	K	W	N	S	M	I	G	A	A
P	W	N	O	F	E	E	E	J	I	Z
Q	S	Y	A	A	U	L	X	V	T	P
F	R	B	B	L	Q	R	A	W	U	K
F	P	V	H	A	Q	Q	H	D	L	R
L	J	O	B	H	Q	A	A	U	L	C
L	S	Z	K	J	T	E	D	A	A	K
D	X	K	X	L	A	S	I	V	H	W
H	U	H	O	H	N	A	K	Z	V	C

AHAD **BAITULLAH** **DUA**

FALAH **HAQQ**

H	J	O	U	T	Y	U	B	K	W	C
D	T	A	Z	P	U	K	A	Z	R	E
I	J	A	I	A	Z	K	K	R	W	G
Y	O	N	G	A	J	M	P	P	B	N
P	L	K	W	N	S	M	I	G	A	A
P	W	N	O	F	E	E	E	J	I	Z
Q	S	Y	A	A	U	L	X	V	T	P
F	R	B	B	L	Q	R	A	W	U	K
F	P	V	H	A	Q	Q	H	D	L	R
L	J	O	B	H	Q	A	A	U	L	C
L	S	Z	K	J	T	E	D	A	A	K
D	X	K	X	L	A	S	I	V	H	W
H	U	H	O	H	N	A	K	Z	V	C

THE SOLUTION

AHAD

literally "one." Islamically, ahad means One Alone, unique, none like God. Al-Ahad is one of the names of God.

BAITULLAH

A mosque, literally "house of God". Specifically means the Ka'aba at Makkah (Mecca

---

DUA

Personal prayer, supplication

FALAH

Deliverance, salvation, well-being.

HAQQ

truth, reality, right, righteousness.
Al-Haqq is one of 99 names of God

Ramadan Day 16

Date: ....

Color in prayer "sajada" for each salah you perform today

Fajr	Duhr	Asr	Maghrib	Isha
2	4	4	3	4

My Quran Tracker

Surah: ....

Verse: .... to: ....
Verse: .... to: ....
Verse: .... to: ....
Verse: .... to: ....
Verse: .... to: ....

My Dhikr Tracker

- ♡ Astaghfirullah: ....
- ♡ Subhan Allah: ....
- ♡ Alhamdulillah: ....
- ♡ la ilaha illa llah: ....
- ♡ Allahu Akbar: ....

My Good Deeds Checklist

- ♡ I Eat Sahour
- ♡ I Say Only Good Things
- ♡ I Make my Parents Happy
- ♡ I Did Dhikr
- ♡ I Give Sadaqah
- ♡ I Keep my Room Tidy
- ♡ I Help Set Up the Table of Iftar
- ♡ I Read Lots About Islam
- ♡ I Read lots of Al-Quran
- ♡ I Prayer on Time

My Fasting Was:

Part · Half · Most · Full

My Thoughts:

....

....

....

....

....

Doodle Challenge for Today

Draw and label 2 Different Kinds of: Biscuits

Activity for Today

Create a mosaic picture

You can find love in the day-to-day

MAZE PUZZLE

Can you find the way to the Masjid

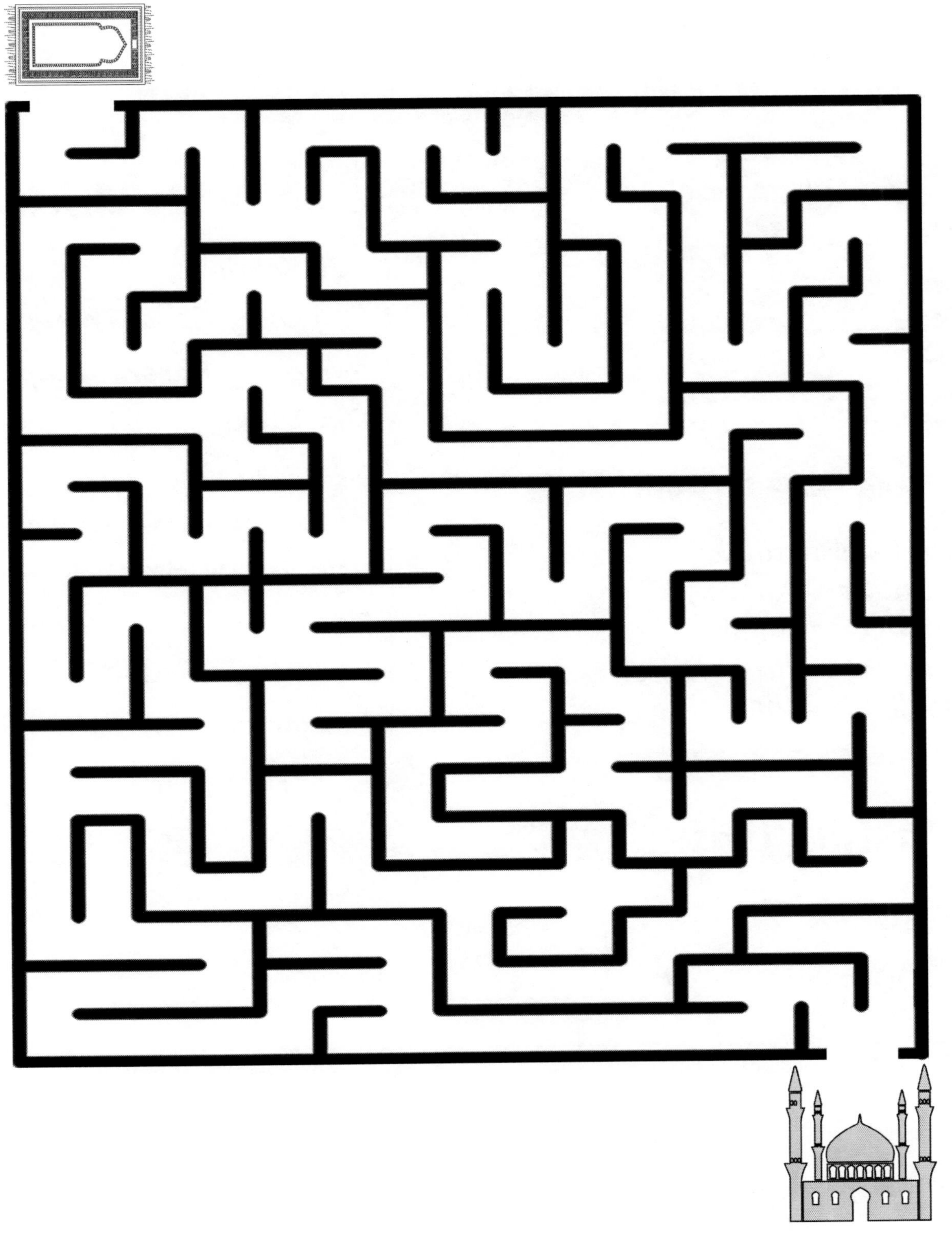

Ramadan Day 17 Date: ....

Color in prayer "sajada" for each salah you perform today

Fajr	Duhr	Asr	Maghrib	Isha
2	4	4	3	4

My Quran Tracker

Surah: ....

Verse: .... to: ....
Verse: .... to: ....
Verse: .... to: ....
Verse: .... to: ....
Verse: .... to: ....

My Dhikr Tracker

- ♡ Astaghfirullah: ....
- ♡ Subhan Allah: ....
- ♡ Alhamdulillah: ....
- ♡ la ilaha illa llah: ....
- ♡ Allahu Akbar: ....

My Good Deeds Checklist

- ♡ I Eat Sahour
- ♡ I Say Only Good Things
- ♡ I Make my Parents Happy
- ♡ I Did Dhikr
- ♡ I Give Sadaqah
- ♡ I Keep my Room Tidy
- ♡ I Help Set Up the Table of Iftar
- ♡ I Read Lots About Islam
- ♡ I Read lots of Al-Quran
- ♡ I Prayer on Time

My Fasting Was: Part Half Most Full

My Thoughts: ....

....

....

....

....

Doodle Challenge for Today

Draw and label 2 Different Kinds of: Writing tools

Activity for Today

learn about Palestine

Word Search

Search and find the five words

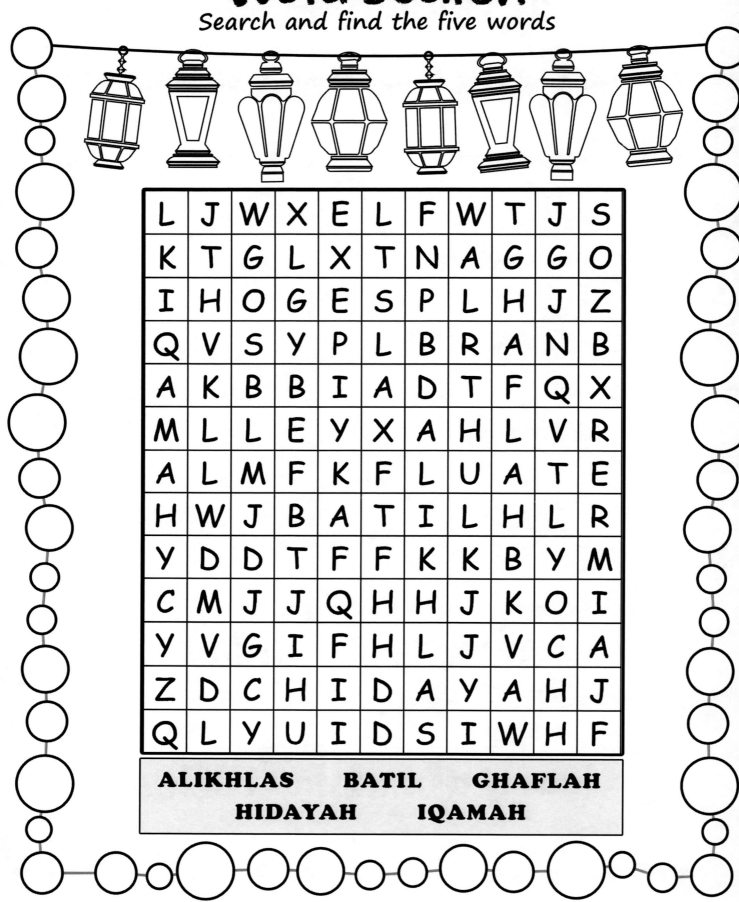

L	J	W	X	E	L	F	W	T	J	S
K	T	G	L	X	T	N	A	G	G	O
I	H	O	G	E	S	P	L	H	J	Z
Q	V	S	Y	P	L	B	R	A	N	B
A	K	B	B	I	A	D	T	F	Q	X
M	L	L	E	Y	X	A	H	L	V	R
A	L	M	F	K	F	L	U	A	T	E
H	W	J	B	A	T	I	L	H	L	R
Y	D	D	T	F	F	K	K	B	Y	M
C	M	J	J	Q	H	H	J	K	O	I
Y	V	G	I	F	H	L	J	V	C	A
Z	D	C	H	I	D	A	Y	A	H	J
Q	L	Y	U	I	D	S	I	W	H	F

ALIKHLAS **BATIL** **GHAFLAH**

HIDAYAH **IQAMAH**

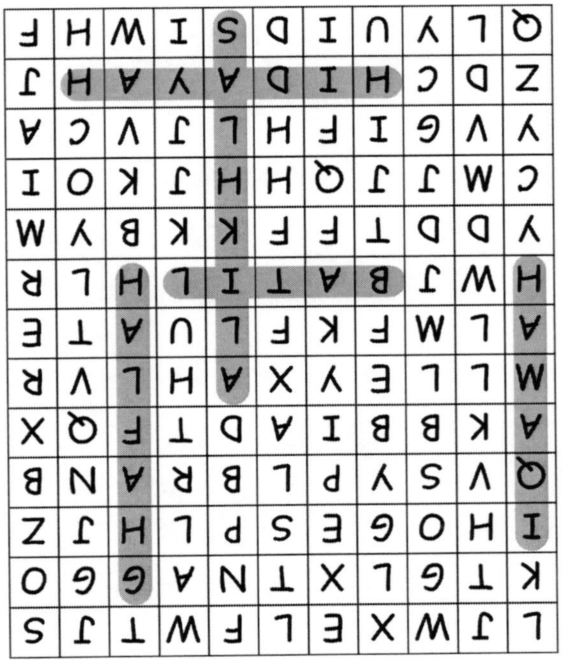

THE SOLUTION

ALIKHLAS

Sincerity and genuineness in religious beliefs

BATIL

Void

GHAFLAH

Heedlessness, forgetfulness of God, indifference

HIDAYAH

Guidance from God.

IQAMAH

The second call to prayer. Similar to the azhan

Ramadan Day 18

Date: ....

Color in prayer "sajada" for each salah you perform today

Fajr	Duhr	Asr	Maghrib	Isha
2	4	4	3	4

My Quran Tracker

Surah: ....

Verse: .... to: ....
Verse: .... to: ....
Verse: .... to: ....
Verse: .... to: ....
Verse: .... to: ....

My Dhikr Tracker

- ♡ Astaghfirullah: ....
- ♡ Subhan Allah: ....
- ♡ Alhamdulillah: ....
- ♡ la ilaha illa llah: ....
- ♡ Allahu Akbar: ....

My Good Deeds Checklist

- ♡ I Eat Sahour
- ♡ I Say Only Good Things
- ♡ I Make my Parents Happy
- ♡ I Did Dhikr
- ♡ I Give Sadaqah
- ♡ I Keep my Room Tidy
- ♡ I Help Set Up the Table of Iftar
- ♡ I Read Lots About Islam
- ♡ I Read lots of Al-Quran
- ♡ I Prayer on Time

My Fasting Was: Part Half Most Full

My Thoughts: ....

Doodle Challenge for Today

Draw and label 2 Different Kinds of: Citrus fruits

Activity for Today

learn about the fruit in the quran

COPY THE PICTURE

	A	B	C	D	E	F
1						
2						
3						
4						
5						
6						
7						
8						

Ramadan Day 19 Date: ....

Color in prayer "sajada" for each salah you perform today

Fajr	Duhr	Asr	Maghrib	Isha
2	4	4	3	4

My Quran Tracker

Surah: ....

Verse: .... to: ....
Verse: .... to: ....
Verse: .... to: ....
Verse: .... to: ....
Verse: .... to: ....

My Dhikr Tracker

- ♡ Astaghfirullah: ....
- ♡ Subhan Allah: ....
- ♡ Alhamdulillah: ....
- ♡ la ilaha illa llah: ....
- ♡ Allahu Akbar: ....

My Good Deeds Checklist

- ♡ I Eat Sahour
- ♡ I Say Only Good Things
- ♡ I Make my Parents Happy
- ♡ I Did Dhikr
- ♡ I Give Sadaqah
- ♡ I Keep my Room Tidy
- ♡ I Help Set Up the Table of Iftar
- ♡ I Read Lots About Islam
- ♡ I Read lots of Al-Quran
- ♡ I Prayer on Time

My Fasting Was:

Part ☆ Half ☆ Most ☆ Full ☆

My Thoughts:

....

Cut and Color this picture

Al Jami Al Umawi

Doodle Challenge for Today

Draw and label 2 Different Kinds of: Planes

Activity for Today

Watch how the blind read the quran in braille

Word Search

Search and find the five words

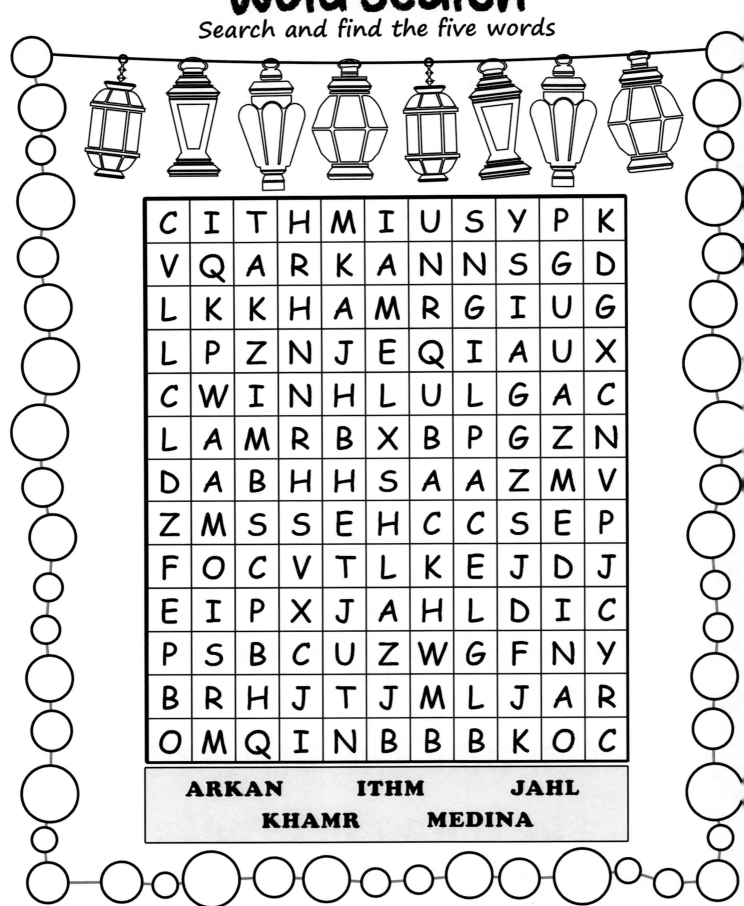

C	I	T	H	M	I	U	S	Y	P	K
V	Q	A	R	K	A	N	N	S	G	D
L	K	K	H	A	M	R	G	I	U	G
L	P	Z	N	J	E	Q	I	A	U	X
C	W	I	N	H	L	U	L	G	A	C
L	A	M	R	B	X	B	P	G	Z	N
D	A	B	H	H	S	A	A	Z	M	V
Z	M	S	S	E	H	C	C	S	E	P
F	O	C	V	T	L	K	E	J	D	J
E	I	P	X	J	A	H	L	D	I	C
P	S	B	C	U	Z	W	G	F	N	Y
B	R	H	J	T	J	M	L	J	A	R
O	M	Q	I	N	B	B	B	K	O	C

ARKAN **ITHM** **JAHL**

KHAMR **MEDINA**

THE SOLUTION

C	I	T	H	M	I	U	S	Y	P	K
V	Q	A	R	K	A	N	N	S	G	D
L	K	K	H	A	M	R	G	I	U	G
L	P	Z	N	J	E	Q	I	A	U	X
C	W	I	N	H	L	U	L	G	A	C
L	A	M	R	B	X	B	P	G	Z	N
D	A	B	H	H	S	A	A	Z	M	V
Z	M	S	S	E	H	C	C	S	E	P
F	O	C	V	T	L	K	E	J	D	J
E	I	P	X	J	A	H	L	D	I	C
P	S	B	C	U	Z	W	G	F	N	Y
B	R	H	J	T	J	M	L	J	A	R
O	W	Q	I	N	B	B	B	K	O	C

ARKAN

The five rukn "pillars" of Islam.

ITHM

The negative reward for bad deeds is tallied on qiyamah (judgment day.) Opposite of thawab

---

JAHL

Ignorance, foolishness.

KHAMR

Intoxicant, wine.

MEDINA

"City"; Medinat-un-Nabi means "the City of the Prophet

Ramadan Day 20 Date: ....

Color in prayer "sajada" for each salah you perform today

Fajr	Duhr	Asr	Maghrib	Isha
2	4	4	3	4

My Quran Tracker

Surah: ....

Verse: .... to: ....
Verse: .... to: ....
Verse: .... to: ....
Verse: .... to: ....
Verse: .... to: ....

My Dhikr Tracker

- Astaghfirullah: ....
- Subhan Allah: ....
- Alhamdulillah: ....
- la ilaha illa llah: ....
- Allahu Akbar: ....

My Good Deeds Checklist

- I Eat Sahour
- I Say Only Good Things
- I Make my Parents Happy
- I Did Dhikr
- I Give Sadaqah
- I Keep my Room Tidy
- I Help Set Up the Table of Iftar
- I Read Lots About Islam
- I Read lots of Al-Quran
- I Prayer on Time

My Fasting Was:

Part Half Most Full

My Thoughts:

....
....
....
....
....

Doodle Challenge for Today

Draw and label 2 Different Kinds of: Gems

Activity for Today

find surah (al-ikhlas) in the quran

Your parent loves you unconditionally

MAZE PUZZLE

Can you call your family and check on them?

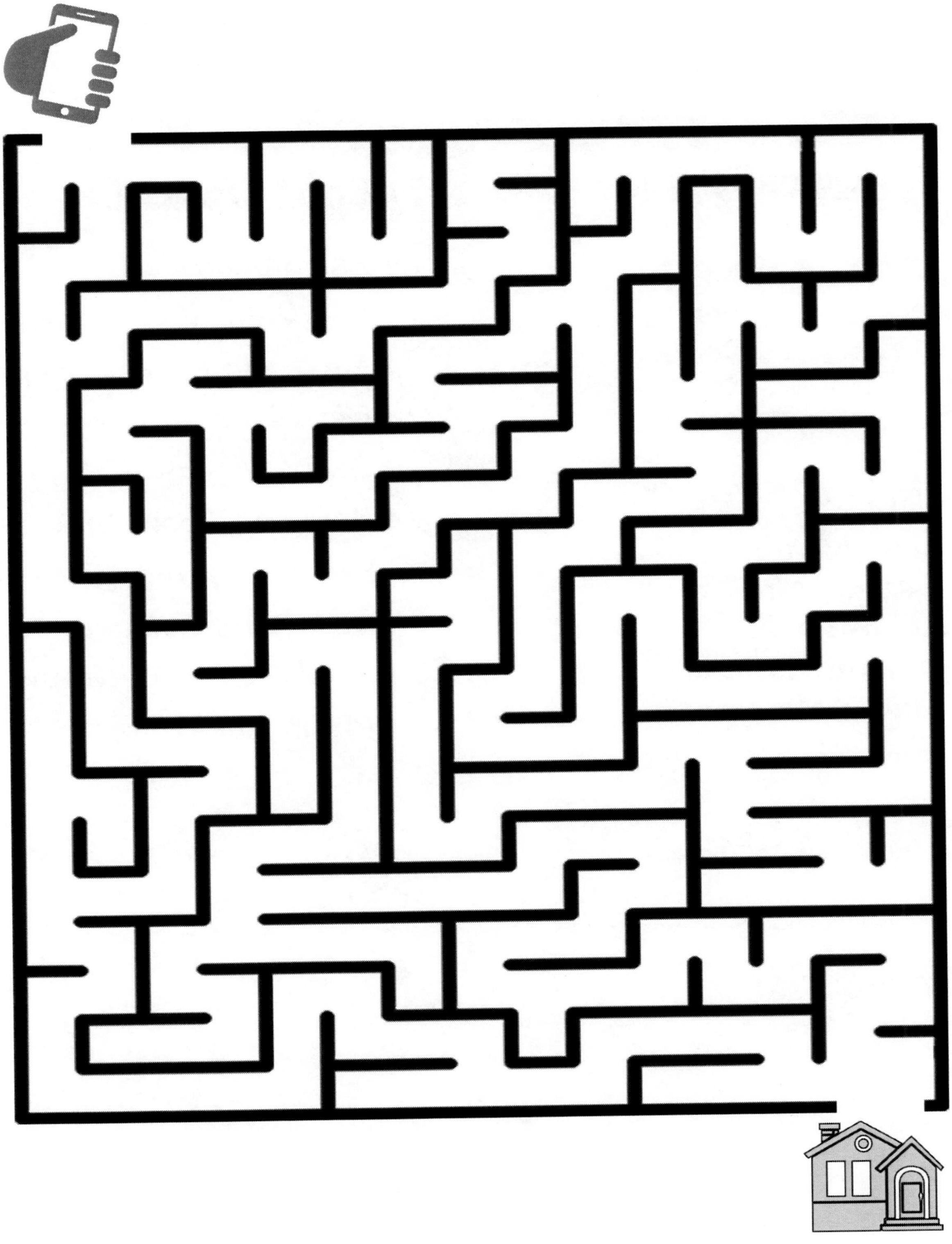

Ramadan Day 21

Date: ....

Color in prayer "sajada" for each salah you perform today

Fajr	Duhr	Asr	Maghrib	Isha
2	4	4	3	4

My Quran Tracker

Surah: ....

Verse: .... to: ....
Verse: .... to: ....
Verse: .... to: ....
Verse: .... to: ....
Verse: .... to: ....

My Dhikr Tracker

- ♡ Astaghfirullah: ....
- ♡ Subhan Allah: ....
- ♡ Alhamdulillah: ....
- ♡ la ilaha illa llah: ....
- ♡ Allahu Akbar: ....

My Good Deeds Checklist

- ♡ I Eat Sahour
- ♡ I Say Only Good Things
- ♡ I Make my Parents Happy
- ♡ I Did Dhikr
- ♡ I Give Sadaqah
- ♡ I Keep my Room Tidy
- ♡ I Help Set Up the Table of Iftar
- ♡ I Read Lots About Islam
- ♡ I Read lots of Al-Quran
- ♡ I Prayer on Time

My Fasting Was:

☆ Part ☆ Half ☆ Most ☆ Full

My Thoughts:

....

....

....

....

....

Doodle Challenge for Today

Draw and label 2 Different Kinds of: House Plants

Activity for Today

Read some (hadiths) about your mom

Word Search

Search and find the five words

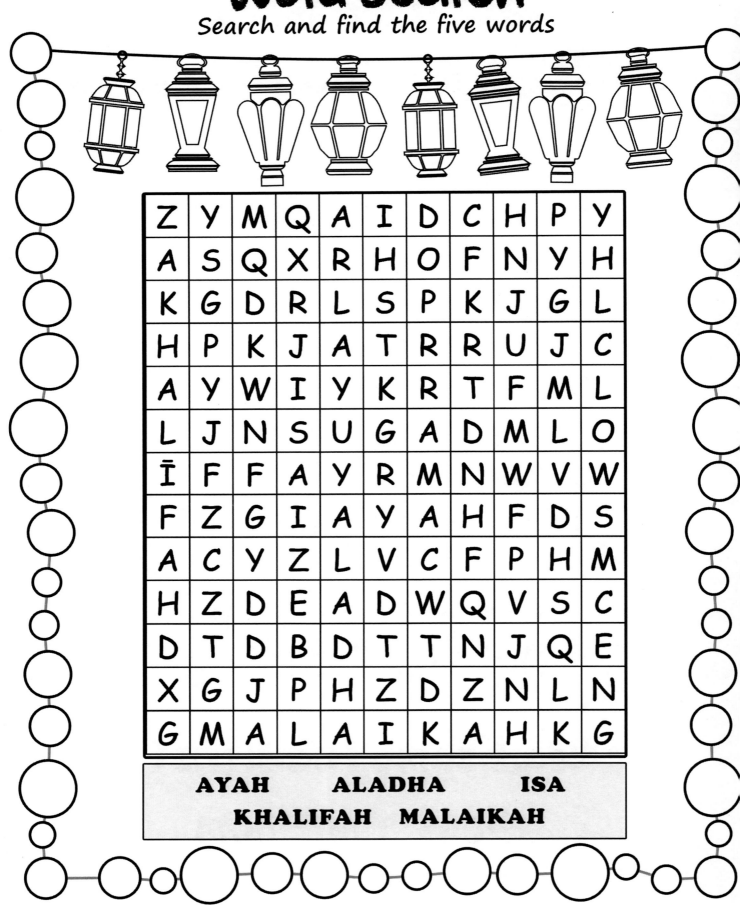

Z	Y	M	Q	A	I	D	C	H	P	Y
A	S	Q	X	R	H	O	F	N	Y	H
K	G	D	R	L	S	P	K	J	G	L
H	P	K	J	A	T	R	R	U	J	C
A	Y	W	I	Y	K	R	T	F	M	L
L	J	N	S	U	G	A	D	M	L	O
Ī	F	F	A	Y	R	M	N	W	V	W
F	Z	G	I	A	Y	A	H	F	D	S
A	C	Y	Z	L	V	C	F	P	H	M
H	Z	D	E	A	D	W	Q	V	S	C
D	T	D	B	D	T	T	N	J	Q	E
X	G	J	P	H	Z	D	Z	N	L	N
G	M	A	L	A	I	K	A	H	K	G

AYAH **ALADHA** **ISA**

KHALIFAH **MALAIKAH**

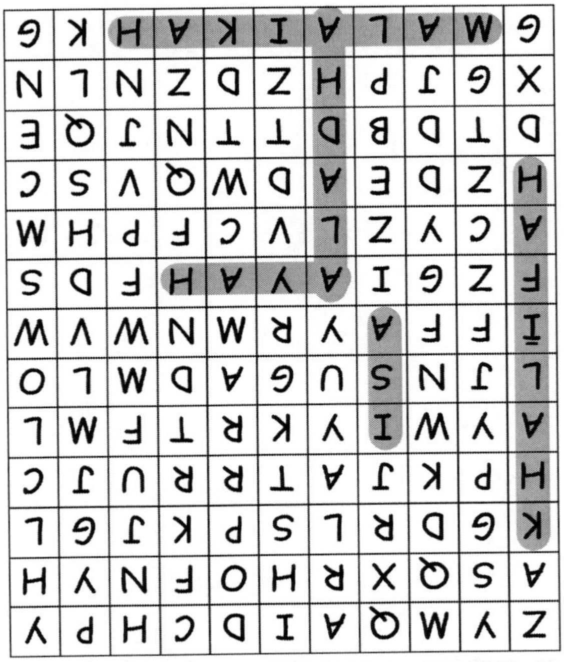

THE SOLUTION

AYAH

A sign. More specifically, a verse in the Qur'an

ALADHA

Honours the willingness of Ibrahim to sacrifice his son Ismael as an act of obedience to God's command.

ISA

Jesus – 'Isa ibn Maryam (English: Jesus son of Mary), (a matronymic since he had no biological father). The Qur'an asserts that Allah has no sons and therefore, 'Isa is not the son of Allah. Muslims honor 'Isa as a nabi and rasul.

KHALIFAH

Caliph, more generally, one performing the duties of khilafa

MALAIKAH

angels (Sing. Malak). Belief in angels is one of the Five Pillars of Islam and requiered for Muslims to believe in

Ramadan Day 22 Date: ....

Color in prayer "sajada" for each salah you perform today

Fajr	Duhr	Asr	Maghrib	Isha
2	4	4	3	4

My Quran Tracker

Surah: ....

Verse: .... to: ....
Verse: .... to: ....
Verse: .... to: ....
Verse: .... to: ....
Verse: .... to: ....

My Dhikr Tracker

- Astaghfirullah: ....
- Subhan Allah: ....
- Alhamdulillah: ....
- la ilaha illa llah: ....
- Allahu Akbar: ....

My Good Deeds Checklist

- I Eat Sahour
- I Say Only Good Things
- I Make my Parents Happy
- I Did Dhikr
- I Give Sadaqah
- I Keep my Room Tidy
- I Help Set Up the Table of Iftar
- I Read Lots About Islam
- I Read lots of Al-Quran
- I Prayer on Time

My Fasting Was:

Part Half Most Full

My Thoughts:

....
....
....
....
....

Doodle Challenge for Today

Draw and label 2 Different Kinds of: Balls

Activity for Today

Make a paper plate cave

A
B
C
D
E
F
1
2
3
4
5
6
7
8

	A	B	C	D	E	F
1						
2						
3						
4						
5						
6						
7						
8						

Ramadan Day 23

Date: ....

Color in prayer "sajada" for each salah you perform today

Fajr	Duhr	Asr	Maghrib	Isha
2	4	4	3	4

My Quran Tracker

Surah: ....

Verse: .... to: ....
Verse: .... to: ....
Verse: .... to: ....
Verse: .... to: ....
Verse: .... to: ....

My Dhikr Tracker

- ♡ Astaghfirullah: ....
- ♡ Subhan Allah: ....
- ♡ Alhamdulillah: ....
- ♡ la ilaha illa llah: ....
- ♡ Allahu Akbar: ....

My Good Deeds Checklist

- ♡ I Eat Sahour
- ♡ I Say Only Good Things
- ♡ I Make my Parents Happy
- ♡ I Did Dhikr
- ♡ I Give Sadaqah
- ♡ I Keep my Room Tidy
- ♡ I Help Set Up the Table of Iftar
- ♡ I Read Lots About Islam
- ♡ I Read lots of Al-Quran
- ♡ I Prayer on Time

My Fasting Was:

☆ Part ☆ Half ☆ Most ☆ Full

My Thoughts:

....

....

....

....

....

Doodle Challenge for Today

Draw and label 2 Different Kinds of: Candle

Activity for Today

Think in a (qadr night) at special dua

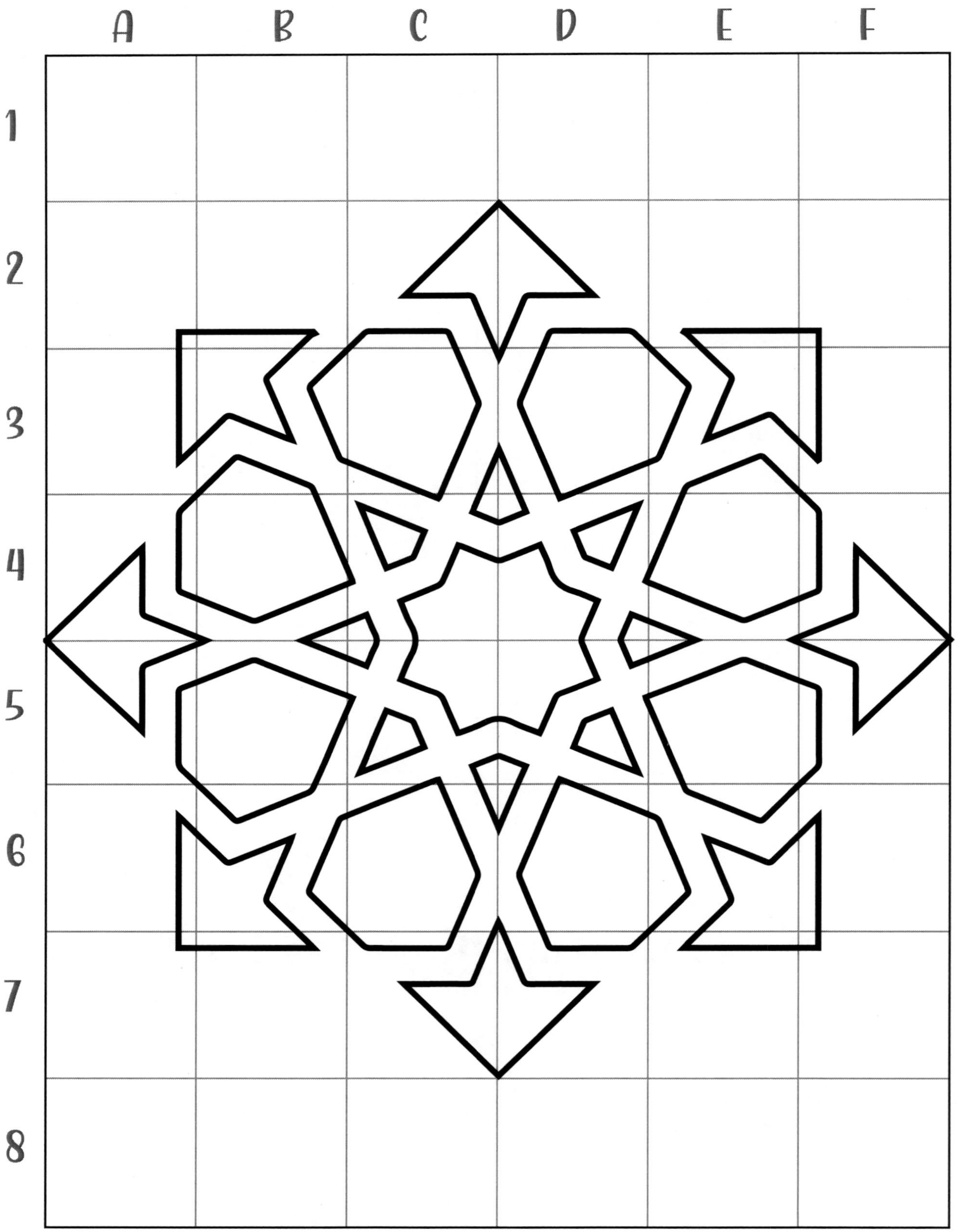
A
B
C
D
E
F
1
2
3
4
5
6
7
8

	A	B	C	D	E	F
1						
2						
3						
4						
5						
6						
7						
8						

Ramadan Day 24 Date: ....

Color in prayer "sajada" for each salah you perform today

Fajr	Duhr	Asr	Maghrib	Isha
2	4	4	3	4

My Quran Tracker

Surah: ....

Verse: .... to: ....
Verse: .... to: ....
Verse: .... to: ....
Verse: .... to: ....
Verse: .... to: ....

My Dhikr Tracker

- ♡ Astaghfirullah: ....
- ♡ Subhan Allah: ....
- ♡ Alhamdulillah: ....
- ♡ la ilaha illa llah: ....
- ♡ Allahu Akbar: ....

My Good Deeds Checklist

- ♡ I Eat Sahour
- ♡ I Say Only Good Things
- ♡ I Make my Parents Happy
- ♡ I Did Dhikr
- ♡ I Give Sadaqah
- ♡ I Keep my Room Tidy
- ♡ I Help Set Up the Table of Iftar
- ♡ I Read Lots About Islam
- ♡ I Read lots of Al-Quran
- ♡ I Prayer on Time

My Fasting Was:

☆ Part ☆ Half ☆ Most ☆ Full

My Thoughts: ....

....

....

....

....

Doodle Challenge for Today

Draw and label 2 Different Kinds of: Berries

Activity for Today

Read the meaning of Surah (laylat al-qadr)

You are good at solving problems

MAZE PUZZLE

Can you help the mother throw the garbage?

Ramadan Day 25 Date: ....

Color in prayer "sajada" for each salah you perform today

Fajr	Duhr	Asr	Maghrib	Isha
2	4	4	3	4

My Quran Tracker

Surah: ....

Verse: .... to: ....
Verse: .... to: ....
Verse: .... to: ....
Verse: .... to: ....
Verse: .... to: ....

My Dhikr Tracker

- ♡ Astaghfirullah: ....
- ♡ Subhan Allah: ....
- ♡ Alhamdulillah: ....
- ♡ la ilaha illa llah: ....
- ♡ Allahu Akbar: ....

My Good Deeds Checklist

- ♡ I Eat Sahour
- ♡ I Say Only Good Things
- ♡ I Make my Parents Happy
- ♡ I Did Dhikr
- ♡ I Give Sadaqah
- ♡ I Keep my Room Tidy
- ♡ I Help Set Up the Table of Iftar
- ♡ I Read Lots About Islam
- ♡ I Read lots of Al-Quran
- ♡ I Prayer on Time

My Fasting Was: Part Half Most Full

My Thoughts: ....

Doodle Challenge for Today

Draw and label 2 Different Kinds of: Orange thing

Activity for Today

learn about word

(la illah ila allah)

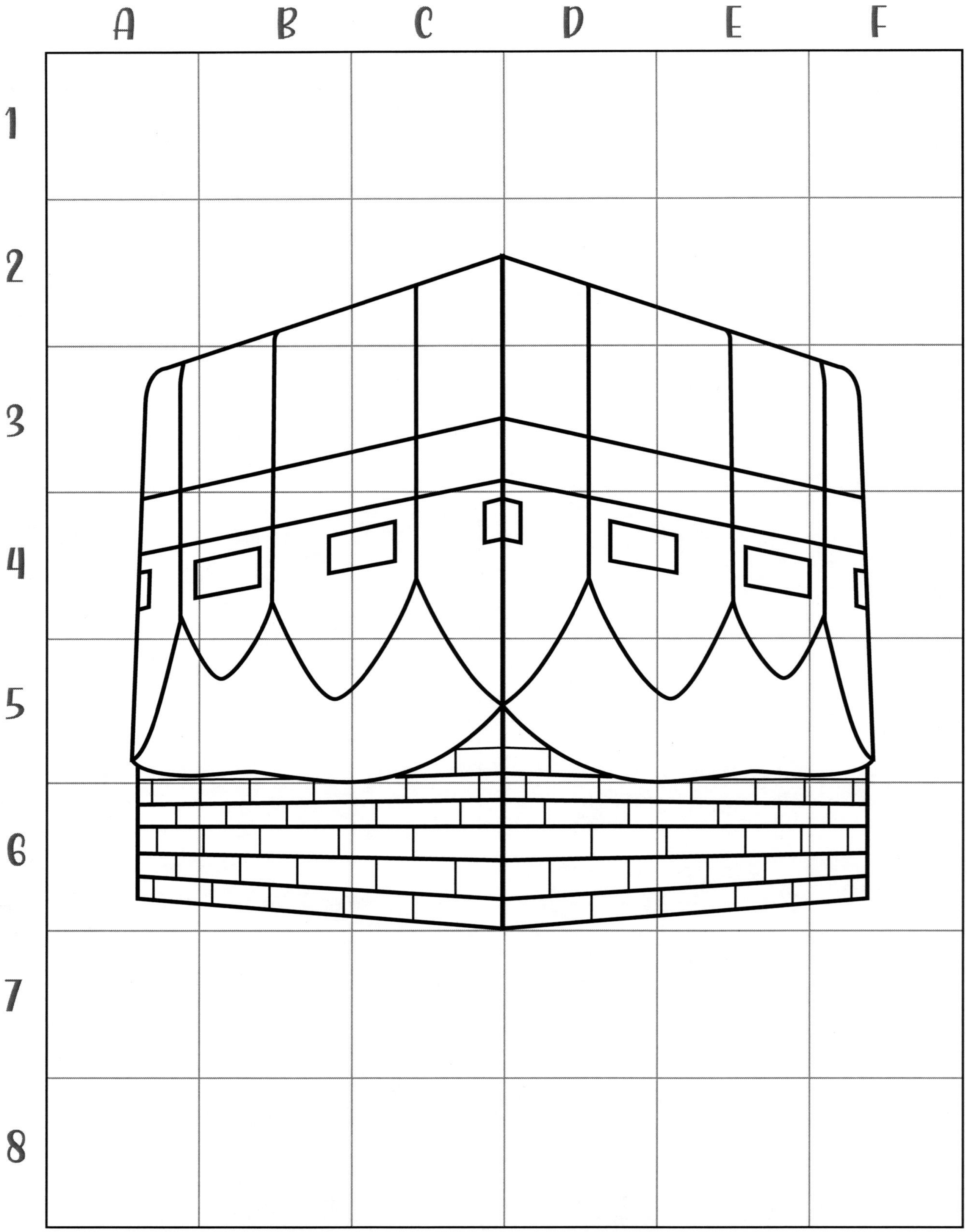
A
B
C
D
E
F
1
2
3
4
5
6
7
8

	A	B	C	D	E	F
1						
2						
3						
4						
5						
6						
7						
8						

Ramadan Day 26 Date: ....

Color in prayer "sajada" for each salah you perform today

Fajr	Duhr	Asr	Maghrib	Isha
2	4	4	3	4

My Quran Tracker

Surah: ....

Verse: .... to: ....
Verse: .... to: ....
Verse: .... to: ....
Verse: .... to: ....
Verse: .... to: ....

My Dhikr Tracker

- Astaghfirullah: ....
- Subhan Allah: ....
- Alhamdulillah: ....
- la ilaha illa llah: ....
- Allahu Akbar: ....

My Good Deeds Checklist

- I Eat Sahour
- I Say Only Good Things
- I Make my Parents Happy
- I Did Dhikr
- I Give Sadaqah
- I Keep my Room Tidy
- I Help Set Up the Table of Iftar
- I Read Lots About Islam
- I Read lots of Al-Quran
- I Prayer on Time

My Fasting Was:

Part Half Most Full

My Thoughts:
....

....

....

....

....

Doodle Challenge for Today

Draw and label 2 Different Kinds of: footprints of pets

Activity for Today

Memories a quranic phrase

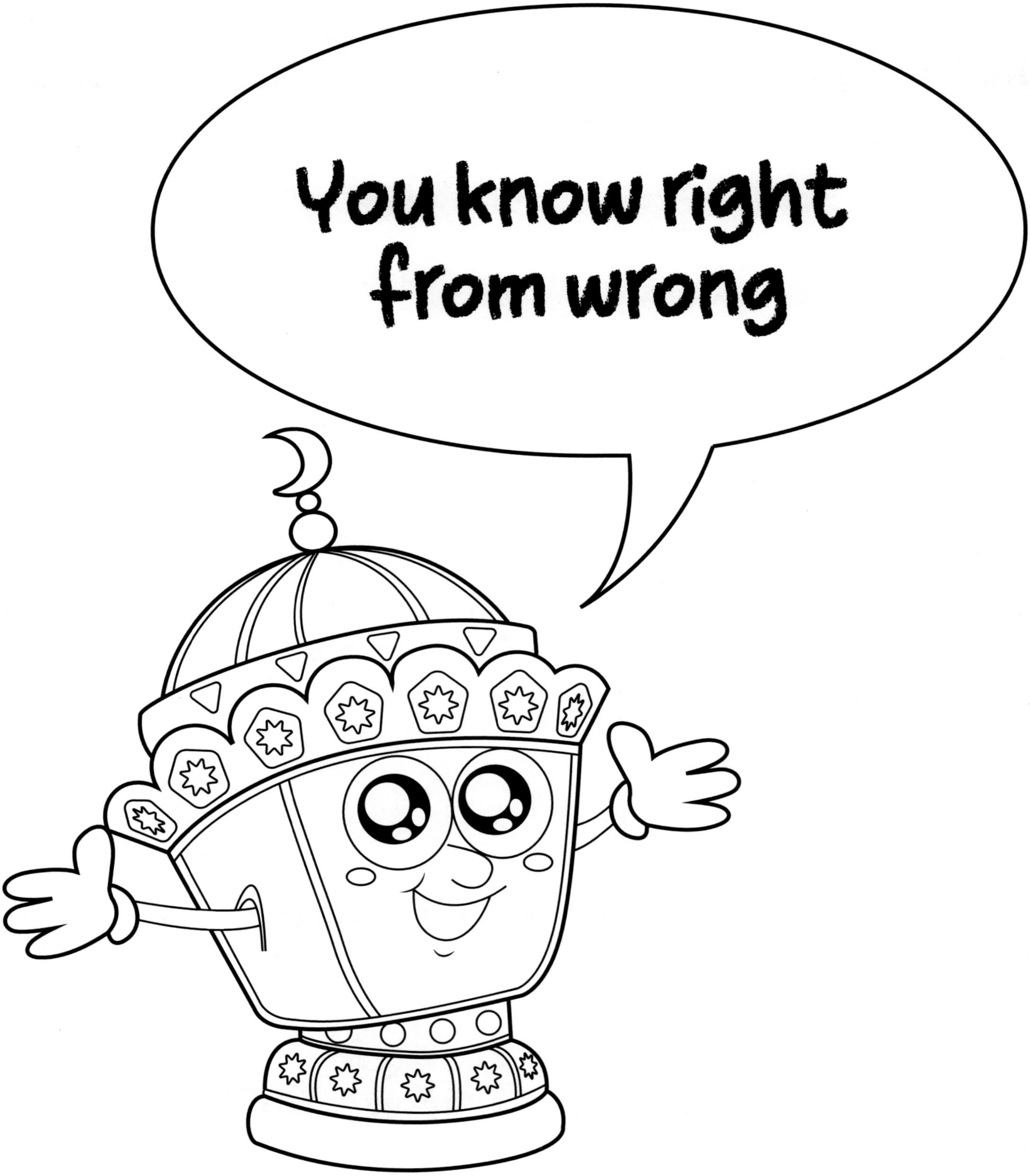
You know right
from wrong

MAZE PUZZLE

Can you feed a poor person?

Ramadan Day 27 Date: ....

Color in prayer "sajada" for each salah you perform today

Fajr	Duhr	Asr	Maghrib	Isha
2	4	4	3	4

My Quran Tracker

Surah: ....

Verse: .... to: ....
Verse: .... to: ....
Verse: .... to: ....
Verse: .... to: ....
Verse: .... to: ....

My Dhikr Tracker

- Astaghfirullah: ....
- Subhan Allah: ....
- Alhamdulillah: ....
- la ilaha illa llah: ....
- Allahu Akbar: ....

My Good Deeds Checklist

- I Eat Sahour
- I Say Only Good Things
- I Make my Parents Happy
- I Did Dhikr
- I Give Sadaqah
- I Keep my Room Tidy
- I Help Set Up the Table of Iftar
- I Read Lots About Islam
- I Read lots of Al-Quran
- I Prayer on Time

My Fasting Was:

Part Half Most Full

My Thoughts:

....

Doodle Challenge for Today

Draw and label 2 Different Kinds of: Book

Activity for Today

Give your mother a flower

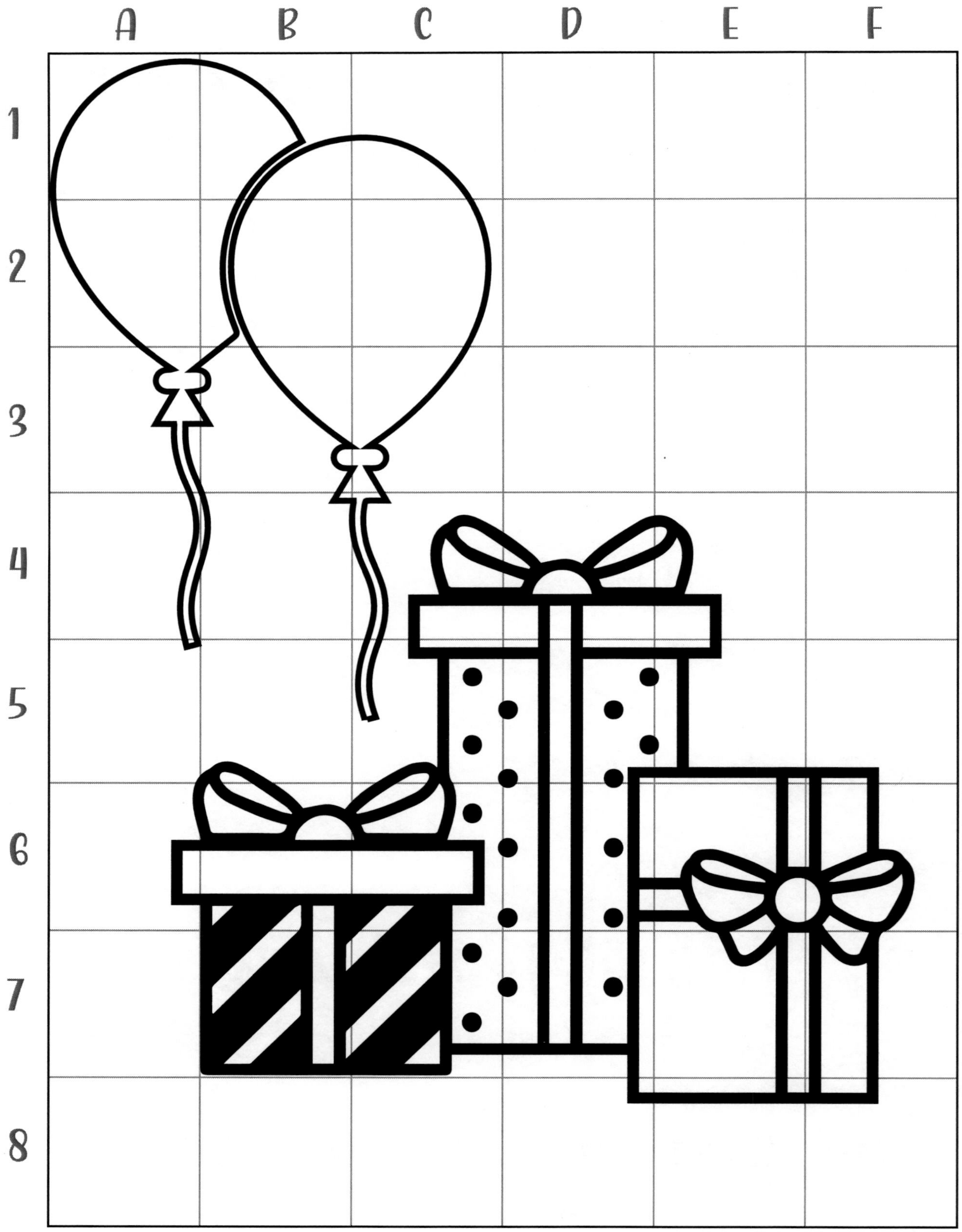
A
B
C
D
E
F
1
2
3
4
5
6
7
8

	A	B	C	D	E	F
1						
2						
3						
4						
5						
6						
7						
8						

Ramadan Day 28

Date: ....

Color in prayer "sajada" for each salah you perform today

Fajr	Duhr	Asr	Maghrib	Isha
2	4	4	3	4

My Quran Tracker

Surah: ....

Verse: .... to: ....
Verse: .... to: ....
Verse: .... to: ....
Verse: .... to: ....
Verse: .... to: ....

My Dhikr Tracker

- ♡ Astaghfirullah: ....
- ♡ Subhan Allah: ....
- ♡ Alhamdulillah: ....
- ♡ la ilaha illa llah: ....
- ♡ Allahu Akbar: ....

My Good Deeds Checklist

- ♡ I Eat Sahour
- ♡ I Say Only Good Things
- ♡ I Make my Parents Happy
- ♡ I Did Dhikr
- ♡ I Give Sadaqah
- ♡ I Keep my Room Tidy
- ♡ I Help Set Up the Table of Iftar
- ♡ I Read Lots About Islam
- ♡ I Read lots of Al-Quran
- ♡ I Prayer on Time

My Fasting Was:

☆ Part ☆ Half ☆ Most ☆ Full

My Thoughts:

....
....
....
....
....

Doodle Challenge for Today

Draw and label 2 Different Kinds of: Flower

Activity for Today

Create a happy eid card

Eid is close

MAZE PUZZLE

Can you contribute to the construction of a Masjid

Ramadan Day 29 Date: ____________

Color in prayer "sajada" for each salah you perform today

Fajr	Duhr	Asr	Maghrib	Isha
2	4	4	3	4

My Quran Tracker

Surah: ____________

Verse: ____________ to: ____________
Verse: ____________ to: ____________
Verse: ____________ to: ____________
Verse: ____________ to: ____________
Verse: ____________ to: ____________

My Dhikr Tracker

- Astaghfirullah: ________
- Subhan Allah: ________
- Alhamdulillah: ________
- la ilaha illa llah: ________
- Allahu Akbar: ________

My Good Deeds Checklist

- I Eat Sahour
- I Say Only Good Things
- I Make my Parents Happy
- I Did Dhikr
- I Give Sadaqah
- I Keep my Room Tidy
- I Help Set Up the Table of Iftar
- I Read Lots About Islam
- I Read lots of Al-Quran
- I Prayer on Time

My Fasting Was:

Part Half Most Full

My Thoughts:

____

____

____

____

____

Cut and Color this picture

Doodle Challenge for Today

Draw and label 2 Different Kinds of: Gift

Activity for Today

Thank Allah for the blessing of Ramadan and Eid

MAZE PUZZLE

Can you help your parents get the Eid gifts?

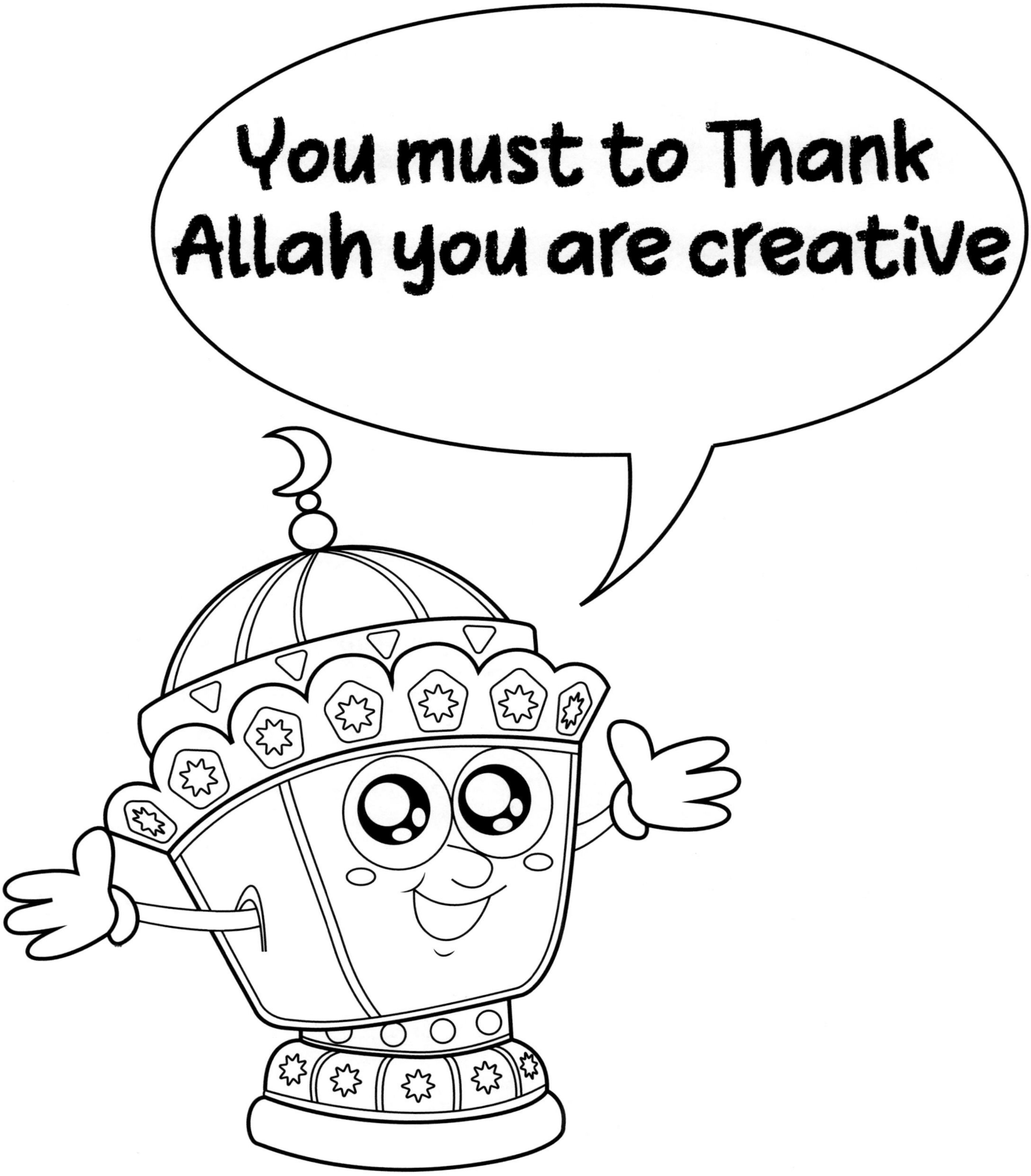
You must to Thank Allah you are creative

Ramadan Day 30 Date: ....

Color in prayer "sajada" for each salah you perform today

Fajr	Duhr	Asr	Maghrib	Isha
2	4	4	3	4

My Quran Tracker

Surah: ....

Verse: .... to: ....
Verse: .... to: ....
Verse: .... to: ....
Verse: .... to: ....
Verse: .... to: ....

My Dhikr Tracker

- ♡ Astaghfirullah: ....
- ♡ Subhan Allah: ....
- ♡ Alhamdulillah: ....
- ♡ la ilaha illa llah: ....
- ♡ Allahu Akbar: ....

My Good Deeds Checklist

- ♡ I Eat Sahour
- ♡ I Say Only Good Things
- ♡ I Make my Parents Happy
- ♡ I Did Dhikr
- ♡ I Give Sadaqah
- ♡ I Keep my Room Tidy
- ♡ I Help Set Up the Table of Iftar
- ♡ I Read Lots About Islam
- ♡ I Read lots of Al-Quran
- ♡ I Prayer on Time

My Fasting Was:

Part Half Most Full

My Thoughts:

....
....
....
....
....

Doodle Challenge for Today

Draw and label 2 Different Kinds of: Sajada

Activity for Today

Give a hug to your family
And tell them Eid Mubarak

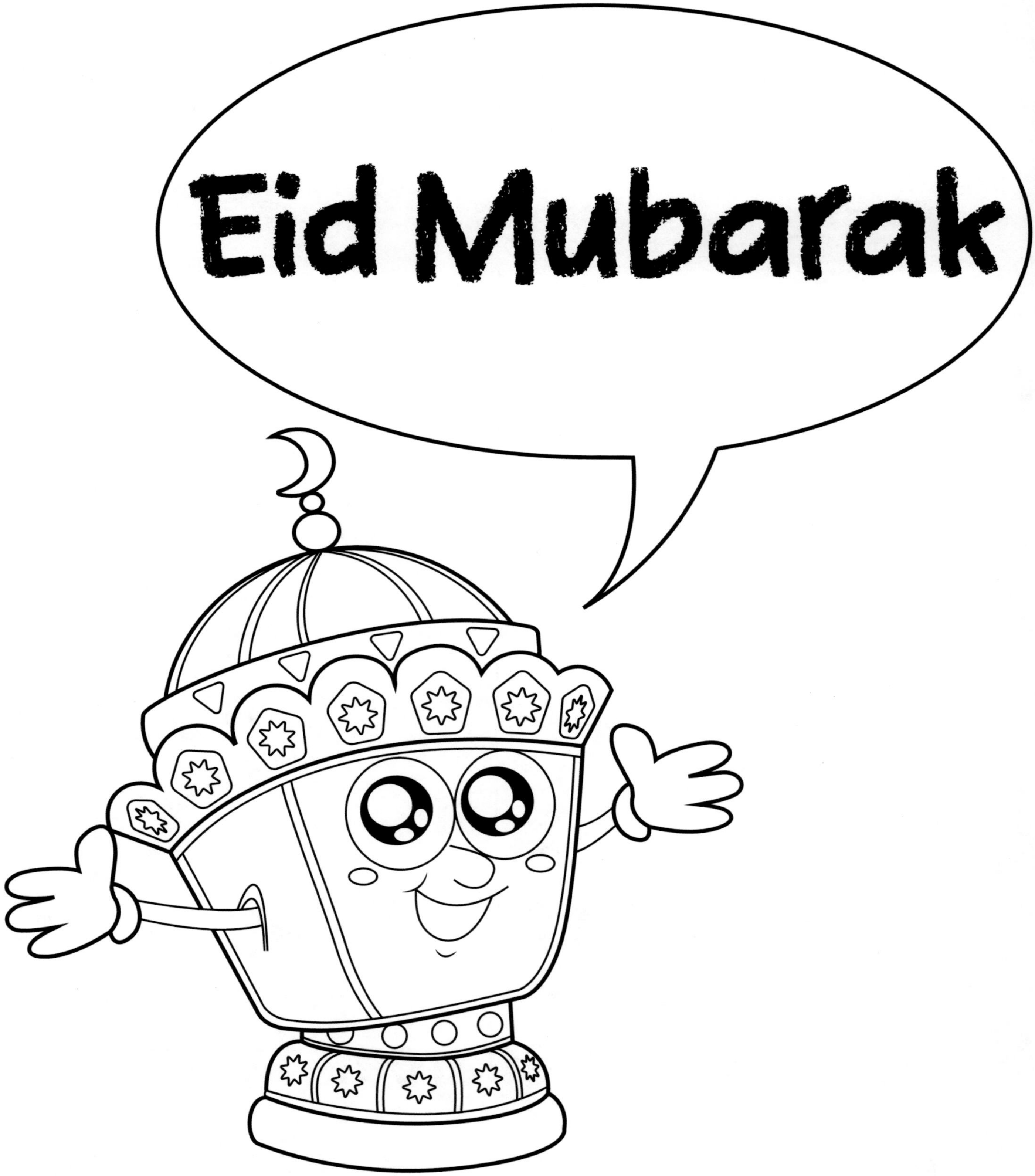
Eid Mubarak

Asalamu alaikum dear

Have you finished the book! I hope you love it,
What do you think about sharing some of your
creations with us on Amazon.

Also, don't forget to support us with a positive review

Thank you very much and good luck

Noor and Aya

Made in United States
Cleveland, OH
27 February 2025

14730441R00077